Ancient Peoples and Places

THE LAPPS

General Editor

DR GLYN DANIEL

Ancient Peoples and Places

THE
LAPPS

Roberto Bosi

29 PHOTOGRAPHS
52 LINE DRAWINGS
AND 3 MAPS

FREDERICK A. PRAEGER

PUBLISHERS

BOOKS THAT MATTER

64 UNIVERSITY PLACE · NEW YORK 3, N. Y.

THIS IS VOLUME SEVENTEEN IN THE SERIES
Ancient Peoples and Places
GENERAL EDITOR: DR GLYN DANIEL

© THAMES AND HUDSON LONDON 1960
THIS IS A REVISED VERSION OF 'I LAPPONI'
TRANSLATED BY JAMES CADELL
© IL SAGGIATORE MILAN 1959
PRINTED IN GREAT BRITAIN
BY THOMAS FORMAN AND SONS LTD NOTTINGHAM
NOT TO BE IMPORTED FOR SALE INTO THE U.S.A.

CONTENTS

ILLUSTRATIONS

General Editor's Preface

THIS IS THE seventeenth volume in the series *Ancient Peoples and Places* which began publication in 1956, and which has, in the last four years, ranged from Scythia to Peru, from the ancient Celts and the Etruscans, to India, Pakistan and Japan. This is the first volume to deal with a living ethnic group. The Lapps today live north of the Arctic circle—in Norway Sweden, Finland and the Kola peninsula of Russia. There are, in all, hardly more than 32,000 of them, and, at present, only between a fifth and a sixth of this number live the traditional life of reindeer herdsmen.

It will be asked why we are devoting a volume in this series to a group of people numbering no more than the inhabitants of the London Borough of Finsbury, and whether we are changing the policy of this series to include modern peoples. The answer to these questions is simple. There are in the world some peoples who, while contemporary with our own society, yet are cultural fossils from an earlier time: they are in fact ancient peoples who have survived to the present day. Such are the Bushmen, and the Gipsies. Such would have been the Tasmanians had they not become extinct in 1876. Such are the Lapps, who may not survive very long as a cultural entity with an Arctic herding economy. Seeing how they live, we may with new eyes look back to the ancient peoples of the Upper Palæolithic and Mesolithic of Europe, without of course falling into the error of supposing that the Lapps are necessarily, or at all, surviving representatives of the Europeans of the Late Ice Age.

This book was first published in Italian, and in editing it for English and American readers, we have had the helpful and expert advice of Dr Ian Whitaker, currently Associate Professor and Head of the Department of Sociology in the Memorial University of Newfoundland.

GLYN DANIEL

Foreword

AMONG THE MANY PERSONS to whom I am indebted for help in my studies of Lapland, I must make special mention of the following: Ernst Manker of the Nordiska Museum of Stockholm, who gave me aid and encouragement more than once, and made it possible for me to meet the Nomads on the occasion of my first travels in Lapland in 1952, besides putting at my disposal all the Museum exhibits; Wilhelm Tawe, parish priest of Jukkasjärvi, who made me welcome in his home even when he himself had to be away for days at a time on parish duties; Fridtjof Rosenlind of Oslo, who got me some very rare books; Pero Casarini who was my companion in one of the 1953 expeditions and provides some of the photographs for this book; the Sunna family of Aitejokk, a Lapp couple who gave me much information on the ancient traditions of their people; and a young Lapp named Mikkel whom I met one September morning south of Kautokeino and with whom I stayed several days, sharing with him a little tent and such few words of his language as I had learned.

ROBERTO BOSI

Introduction

FRANCESCO NEGRI, the priest from Ravenna, has left us a good description of Lapland towards the close of the seventeenth century. He opens Letter 1 of his 'Northern Journey'[1] with these words:

'A vast land, extending more than a thousand Italian miles: a people without bread of any kind, made either by their own hand or others'; for no oats can grow there and the land is like-wise deprived of all fruit, trees and crops, for these need soil. Domestic animals such as are found in the rest of the world are unknown here. In a country denied even grass, what could they feed on? Needless to say, milk and eggs are lacking too. No vines are there to provide men with drink, nor can any brew be made from grain, there being none. In a word, nought can take root here, and no product can be gathered. So that there is furthermore no wool, nor flax for men's clothing. I will not say there are no cities in this land. Houses themselves do not exist. Of all such is this land deprived. Nor are its blessings any com-fort for its lack! One night in this region may last no less than two months, and yet more, according to where the traveller halts. The cold is of such rigour that for eight months of the year snow and ice cover all land and all water. And these may in part remain two months more, so that only July and August are free from winter's grip. On the higher mountains lies an unchanging snow-cap, and to a depth of a foot or two feet beneath the ground, frost prevails. In many a marshy place, you may find ice throughout every season; while as for summer, the air is noxious with mosquitoes and midges which come in such hosts that the sun is obscured. All this being so, one would surely hold that the country cannot be inhabited by so much as

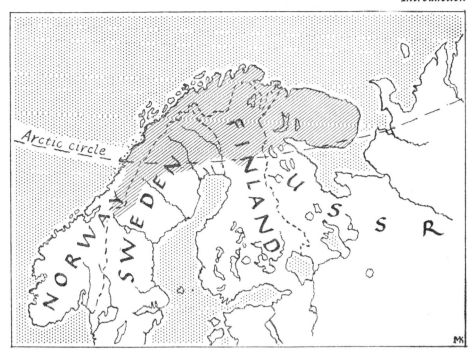

Fig. 1. Map showing the distribution of the Lapps at the present time

wild beasts. It must surely be a desert. Yet inhabited it is. For this land, Illustrious Lord, is none other than the land I speak of – Lapland.'

In this wild region, which Negri has painted in such sombre colours, the Lapps still live today. There are at present some 32,000 of them. In the more southerly districts there are some who have settled down in one place and become, in a humble way, an agricultural society. The rest remain nomads, or semi-nomads, following their reindeer into the trackless uplands of the north.

Like many other peoples, they do not give themselves the name the world knows them by. They prefer one whose origin is obscure: *Sabme.*

Lapp, Lopar – some such name has always been given to them by neighbouring peoples, and it is capable of various interpretations, dictated more often than not by the particular anthropological and ethnological theory favoured by the interpreter. One school of thought sees an Asiatic origin in this northern people; so it avers that 'Lapp' is derived from the Mongolian 'lu⁄pe', meaning 'going towards the north'. But others, who make the Lapps share their dim beginnings with the Finns, have hunted up two words of archaic Finnish: 'lappes', with the most appropriate meaning of 'banished', and 'lapu' signifying either 'uttermost limit' or 'witch'. It is a case where 'doctors disagree'. But at least there can be no doubt about the existence of a folk designated as Lapps, or something similar. They are the people who from time immemorial have lived on the extreme fringe of Europe in a land whose northern boundary is only marked by the Arctic Ocean.

There are yet others who trace the name Lapp back to the Swedish word for 'rags and tatters', the reference being to the ragged clothing they often wore. Or to the Swedish verb, 'löpa' – to run – (like the German *laufen*). Lapps of all ages have certainly shown exceptional skill in the use of skis. In all probability, they invented them.

So it may well be that this last derivation comes closest to the truth.

Today, the Lapps are spread over an enormous region extending from the Atlantic coast of Norway to the Kola peninsula in the USSR – living, for the most part, beyond the Arctic Circle, but all the time feeling their way more and more southwards, especially in Swedish territory. Some are the subjects of Norway or Sweden, others of Finland or Russia. The great majority of Lapps are to be found in Norway, especially in Finnmark, its most northerly province. In Finnmark there are some 20,000 of them. For Sweden, a recent census has given the figure of 8,500. There are reckoned to be 2,300 in

Finland, and 1,800 in the USSR. In Norway, reindeer-breeding Lapps are nowadays few and far between, and they are seldom to be encountered except along the coasts and the rivers. They live by fishing and hunting, and by following a few crafts. In Sweden there is a difference between mountain-Lapps and forest-Lapps. The former still largely preserve the nomadic traditions of the ancient reindeer-herding culture; they migrate with the seasons from plain to upland pastures, and back from the upland pastures to the plain. The forest-Lapps, keeping their herds in the depths of dense woodland belts, make only a few migrations, and these only of a localized character. Finnish and Russian Lapps, for the most part, also maintain their herds in forested regions.

In numbers, the Lapps have scarcely varied since the eighteenth century, though latterly, after a slight setback, there may have been some increase. Although it is a common belief that they are dying out there is no justification for this view. It is true, however, that the ancient Lapp culture is slowly being crowded out by modern civilization. The tents and cabins are far less often seen today, and then only among the real nomad element. The old racial festivals are being forgotten. National costume, for all too many Lapps, is becoming something to put on for the benefit of the summer tourists. But up in the mountains of the north, a great deal of the really ancient tradition is still to be seen: in that harsh region, whole families still live off the reindeer, and the reindeer alone, whilst the only habitation they know is a tent. The reindeer give them food, drink, their pelts for a bed and clothing, their bones and horns for household utensils; on top of all that, they provide them with swift transport across the frozen wastes.

Spread out so thin over a territory so vast – a back-of-beyond consisting of sea-coast and mountain – it is small wonder that the Lapps have passed for a people of exiles, driven back on to the very fringes of the habitable world. As we have just seen, this belief gave rise to one etymological theory as to the origin of their very name.

The language they speak today belongs to the Finno-Ugric branch of the Uralic family. There may be some linguistic relation between Lappish, Finnish, Esthonian, Hungarian and the tongues of the Voguls, Ostyaks, Zyryans, the Cheremiss people and the Mordvins; these last five are hunting and fishing folk surviving from the remotest times in USSR territory.

In the past, affinities have been established between the Lappish and the Altaic – that is, Turko-Mongolian – languages. But any such relationship is nowadays discounted. Indeed, the most recent research rules it out. On the other hand there would appear to be clear proof of kinship with certain Yukaghir patois spoken in North-east Asia by groups of reindeer hunters known as 'Palæo-Siberian'. The linguistic roots go back a long way. But is the language spoken by the Lapps of today their original tongue? We can be by no means sure. The Lapps owe a great part of their culture to the Finnish tribes, who have been their neighbours for centuries. If ever they had some archaic tongue of their own, no trace of it remains now. According to research carried out by the Swede Wiklund,[2] the Finnish language was adopted by the Lapps – or forced upon them perhaps – about the beginning of the Christian era.

The fact is that quite a few dialects are spoken in Lapland, and the difference between them can be considerable. In the Kola peninsula, the patois shows a good deal of Russian influence. But it still preserves its link with the Inari dialect of Lapps living in the neighbourhood of Lake Inari in Finland. This is generally known as 'Eastern Lappish'. Then there is the 'Northern Lappish' spoken in Norwegian Finnmark, in the Swedish districts of Lake Torneträsk and the Swedish-Finnish frontier. Two rather more southern versions, very close to each other, are used in the zones of Luleå and Piteå in

Sweden. Lastly, we have 'Southern Lappish' proper, spoken in central Norway, and, in Sweden, round Västerbotten, Jämtland, Härjedalen, and Dalecarlia (Dalarna); there is considerable Swedish influence here.

PART ONE

DISCOVERING A PEOPLE

CHAPTER I

The Reindeer-Hunters

To THE WEST of the Ural Mountains, in the plain between the River Khama – a tributary of the Volga – and the hilly uplands where the Oka and the Moskowa rise, many groups of hunters were to be found at the close of the last Ice Age. Their prey was reindeer, fallow-deer, wild boar, otter and wild dog. The day came when they learned to tame the ferocious dogs as puppies, making sure that they grew up faithful and obedient. From that day on, the other animals had two enemies – not man alone, but also the dog who had been taught to serve him at his hunting.

Today, when we come upon the remains of these hunters, we may well find beside them the bones of the dogs they had kept for hunting – in the wild Russian plain, in Poland, in the Carpathians, in the Baltic, and even farther westwards. Those tribes, too, which dwelt in the great solitudes stretching to the east of the Urals, had learned to breed these animals, and highly useful they proved for transport across the snow. At Krasno-jarsk on the banks of the Yenisei in Siberia, the bones of a dog were discovered on the site of an ancient encampment. Clearly he had been a draught animal, since remnants of his trappings were found too.

Here is proof that among the Arctic populations the dog was harnessed to the sled before the reindeer. In Finnish peat-bogs, the runners of sledges dating back to the Early Stone Age, the Palæolithic Era, have come to light. Europe's most ancient traces of the dog, which would seem to be the first domesticated animal, were discovered during excavations at Maglemöse, on the south coast of the Baltic. They were pro-nounced to be of Mesolithic origin – that is, dating from the transition between the Early Stone Age and the later one –

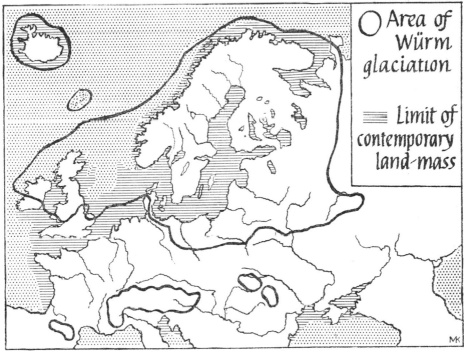

Fig. 2. Map showing maximum expansion of ice in the Würm glaciation

from the period intermediate in time between the Palæolithic and the Neolithic.

These Ice Age hunters made use of the less rigorous seasons of the year to build up food supplies to tide them and their families over the others. They had to be nomads: they had to move with the seasonal moves of the animal kingdom. If the animals made some special migration, they had to follow. But there was one more very weighty argument against their settling down in one place: the reindeer, their main source of food and skins, showed a tendency to migrate slowly north-wards all the time. Thus, a day may have come when these primitive hunters thought it advisable to call a halt to their relentless northward trek. They seem to have pinned their

Fig. 2

hopes on fish for a while instead of reindeer. They established fixed camps wherever the yield was good. But then the fish too, for some unknown reason, began to migrate in their turn.

Over a long period, these hunters lived in the tundra-lands which had come to cover Northern Europe, and part of Central Europe with the ending of the last climatic cold phase, which is represented by a belt of birch-trees on the southern Baltic coast with their trunks bent towards the south, weighed down by the advancing ice-mass. Radio-carbon analysis gave the age of such remains of plant-life as about 11,000 years, a figure that is borne out by analysis of remains in other regions.

From that time on, the heat of the sun began to melt the ice. The packed snow split up and torrents gushed forth. Rivers burst their banks, turning plains into lakes, and salmon migrated in search of new waters for spawning. At first it looked as if the world were turning into one huge marsh. Then, slowly, forest began to take command, and man had a new kind of game to hunt. Mammoth and musk-oxen multiplied and grew to formidable numbers. Now, of the ancient fauna, only reindeer and bison remained. They grazed in great herds on the outer fringes of the wooded belts, in the borderland between forest and tundra.

Man soon became aware that the reindeer herds were inclined to keep moving northwards, in search of the lichen to be found in regions where snow was still frequent. Both in Europe and in Asia, indeed, all along the arc of those tundra-lands which had formed where the ice had melted, the hunters were faced with a grave problem. Their food was moving northward, and new, warlike tribes were pressing up from the south into areas now clear of snow. In Asia, where no glaciation existed on the same vast scale as in Europe, the tundra-dwellers were very quick to set out. In Europe the northward trek was a slower business. To this very day, traces of these hunting-peoples can be found between the Urals and the

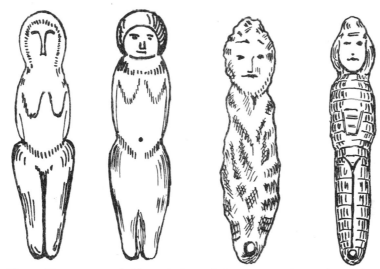

Fig. 3. Four statuettes, datable to the later Aurignacian Age, discovered at Maltá, Siberia

Upper Volga, and along the eastern arc of the Baltic; as also between Lake Ladoga and Lake Onega. Human destiny was now precariously linked to the migratory instincts of the animal kingdom.

Excavations have been carried out at Gagarino on the banks of the Don in the USSR, at Mezin in the vicinity of Kiev and farther north at Elissevici. All point to the same thing: a rough cultural uniformity among these reindeer-hunting people, along this entire land-belt. It is underlined by the similarity of such household chattels as have come to light at many places scattered over the great central plain of Europe, for instance: Předmost, Brno, Pekárna and Dolní Věstonice in Czecho-slovakia; Willendorf in Austria; Oberkassel, Petersfeld, Ander-nach, Vogelherd, Balver Höhle and Ahrensburg in Germany – and so on, into Belgium, Switzerland and France, where there are all those famous names in the Dordogne (Laugerie, Les

Fig. 3

27

Eyzies, La Madeleine, etc.), and in the Pyrenees (Brassempouy, Lespugue, Tuc d'Audoubert, Les Trois Frères, Mas d'Azil, etc.). Yet in Moravia and the Ukraine this celebrated decora⁄tive art of the Palæolithic Age assumes variant charac⁄teristics: there is a certain deviation from the great Western European art⁄stream; though, in fact, in Moravia we find some evidence of a merging of the cultural elements of the great sub⁄glacial belt. There we encounter both the 'naturalism' of the Dordogne and of the Pyrenees, and the geometrical designs, very definitely ornamental, inspired by the purely geometrical figures of Mezin (Kiev) and the stylistic elements evoking the Bureti and Maltá locations on Lake Baikal. So much for the Asiatic aspects of the sub⁄glacial culture which culminated in the Magdalenian at the end of the Ice Age; they owe their fame to their survival, with all their peculiar characteristics, through periods of great change in climate and population. As for individual items of material culture, close analysis of the dis⁄coveries made in various regions leads us to conclude that this great sub⁄glacial culture was founded on a tradition of hunting and man's consequent dependence upon animals for the necessities of existence. After the great Magdalenian epoch, which covers the last millennia of the Palæolithic Age, man became completely preoccupied with the extraordinary climatic developments then taking place. Domestic art and rock⁄drawing too became rarer, a contributory factor being the expansion of the sub⁄glacial populations over a very wide area in a very short time.

The deep valleys of the Volga and the Dnieper have yielded huge quantities of reindeer bones and sometimes, in equal pro⁄fusion, the remains of wild horses – telling proof of the use the hunters made of a hill overlooking a river to capture a large herd, and then to destroy it. The sites of these reindeer cemeteries suggest two methods of ambush on the part of man. Once the herd was sighted, the hunters might drive it into a gorge formed by two high walls of rock, or the narrows of a stream, where it became a helpless target for the swiftest arrows of the tribe. Or they might try and force the animals into a deep ravine formed by some great river; in such a case the whole herd would dash itself to death.

Furthermore, the reindeer has always taken a delight in heading for some narrow passage where the icy wind blows all the keener into the muzzle. Man was well aware of this, and he knew where to lie in wait. Enormous piles of reindeer bones, discovered in the heaped loess of regions which subsequently became the steppe, often indicate that the site of some ancient encampment is close at hand.

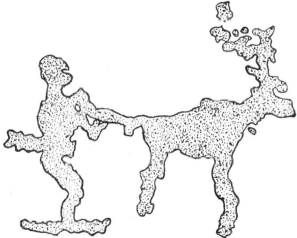

Fig. 4. Cave-drawing of a figure on skis drawn along by a reindeer, at Zalavrouga, on the White Sea, USSR

All the evidence points to the fact that at some stage in man's history, the reindeer-hunters occupied a vast semicircle stretching across Central and Eastern Europe, and also beyond the Urals: and it is precisely at the moment of maximum expansion among these hunting-peoples that our problem arises – the problem of the origin of the Lapps – the most ancient extant race in Europe, and the only one to have conserved some traces at least of the old reindeer-herding culture.

The mighty northward trek of the reindeer started from the plains of Russia and the Baltic, and followed the one route by which the far north of Europe could be reached – in spite of apparent obstacles in the shape of the two lakes, Ladoga and Onega, shutting off their access to Karelia. And it is just in the neighbourhood of these lakes that we find traces of a hunting-people who followed the herds. Pasturage and climate suited the reindeer's needs, and we may be certain that in this region the hunters stayed for a considerable time.

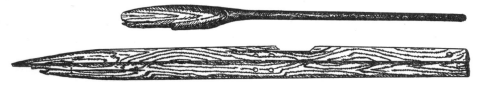

Fig. 5. Ski and spade-type ski-stick found in a marsh near Kalvträsk, Sweden. This type of ski-stick was probably used by reindeer-breeders to clear away the snow to enable the reindeer to get to the lichen. At present in the Länsmuseum at Umea

It was at this stage that man tried to exert some control over the roving reindeer – ever drawn towards the cold, bracing breezes from the snow-clad hills. He herded the beasts into enclosures, and helped them to breed by protecting them, when the time for birth came, from their natural enemies – among them, the wolf, the wolverine (or glutton) and the eagle. As a result of this, the idea of taming the reindeer must have occurred to him.

For a long time, scholars argued that this process could only have happened in the region occupied at this period by the Lapps, in view of the ideally suitable geographical and climatic conditions which prevailed there. But if we examine the study made by W. J. Raudonikas of rock-drawings found near Lake

Fig. 4.

30

Onega and near the White Sea,[1] we shall see how these primitive graffiti, dating back to the so-called 'comb ceramic' period of ornamental work on stone, may well refer to a tradition of reindeer-breeding already in existence. Formerly they were held to illustrate only hunting scenes, thereby suggesting that at the time man's skill had not advanced beyond the hunting stage.

It is worth noting, furthermore, that the ski-sticks discovered in various zones may have a second purpose which was overlooked in the past, and which supports the theory that, during

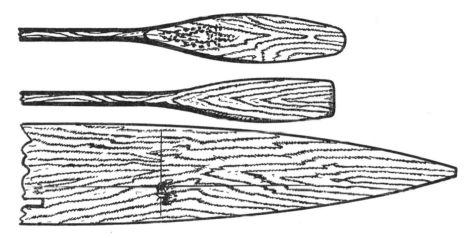

Fig. 6. Two small spades and a ski, as in use among the Ostyaks in the last century

the latter stages of this northward trek, some groups of hunters ceased to be merely hunters, and became reindeer-breeders. For one end of these ski-sticks was fashioned like a spade, and this may well have been for the purpose of clearing the snow to get at the lichen for the reindeer's grazing. A wooden implement of this type was unearthed at Västerbotten, Sweden, near Kalvträsk, and analysis by the pollen method put its age at about 4,000 years. The shape is the same as that encountered

Fig. 5

31

Fig. 6

within historical times among the Samoyeds and the Ostyaks. This discovery affords, however, no irrefutable proof that rein/deer were bred at this time, as opposed to being merely hunted. It certainly points to the fact that even in that epoch of pre/history, hunters inhabiting the tundra between Lake Ladoga

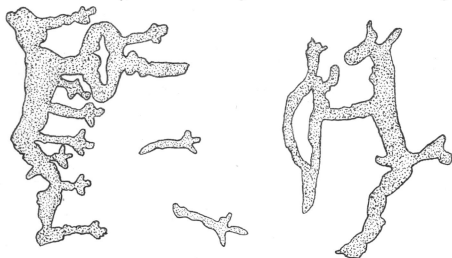

Fig. 7. Figures in a cave-drawing at Zalavrouga, on the White Sea, USSR, representing shamans wearing masks. One is shooting arrows at the other, and the implement being held out in self-defence is probably a sacred drum. The scene may illustrate some ancient sacrificial ritual which has disappeared without trace

and Lake Onega had moved on in no uncertain fashion to/wards the territory which is now Lapland.

Unremitting search by the Swede Ernst Manker has enabled us to make quite an advance towards the solution of our prob/lem. Manker states[2] that the most ancient documents on rein/deer/breeding relate to the period round A.D. 500; and he makes much of the folklore of the region near Lake Baikal, from which region we have information about the Soyot and the Tungus peoples living in the Irkutsk district of Siberia. That is not to say that reindeer/breeding went unknown and un/practised in more westerly zones, even though documentary evidence in Europe does not begin until about the ninth century. This date was arrived at after the most conscientious study. An earlier one, therefore, though its possibility cannot be ruled out, would need archaeological evidence to support and confirm it.

It is important for us to know at what period the domestication of animals got under way, because then we might have an approximate date for the settlement of the Lapps in Scandinavia. The domestication of the reindeer herds on a large scale was probably first achieved on Scandinavian soil. Utensils, bones, and horns, discovered by excavation, provide us with clues and sometimes with definite evidence. The age of the Kalvträsk ski-stick – 4,000 years – confirms a date already attributed to the rock-drawings and, taken in conjunction with similar examples which have come to light, does afford some proof of a uniform type of culture extending over Arctic territory in prehistoric times.

Manker very properly brings out the point that skis were less necessary to the hunter than to the herdsman, who followed the reindeer in the course of long journeys. It is interesting to note in this connection that the Palæo-Siberians – hunters of reindeer, and not breeders – lacked the ski in prehistoric and historic times alike, though they had devised the racket-shoe and the snow-shoe, which they used to an enormous extent.

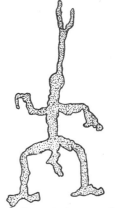

Fig. 8. Rock-drawing of a dancing shaman, wearing masks and horns, discovered at Peri-Noss, on Lake Onega, USSR

Whatever may be the manner in which the first phase of the reindeer-herding culture arose, we know that a sizeable nucleus of reindeer-hunters of the ancient pattern remained for a long period in the tundra between Lake Ladoga and Lake Onega, later pushing northward to follow on after an essentially hunting culture. When did these peoples reach Scandinavia?

At Zalavrouga, on the White Sea, there are carvings and paintings which tell us of other highly important aspects of the culture of these hunters who followed the reindeer as it moved north. At least three of the figures depicted can be interpreted with certainty as magicians or 'shamans'. They appear in their

C

Fig. 9. *Masked witch-figure, dancing, from a cave-painting at Les Trois Frères, Ariège, France*

role of intermediary between the people and the animals hunted – between the hunter's hunger and his food. What we see are human figures with animal heads; in two cases the headdress takes the form of a reindeer's antlered head, while in a third, the nose is of a length so disproportionate as to suggest a muzzle. One of these figures holds some object which it is probably safe to identify as a drum, of a type still in use to this day among the shamans of Siberia and to be seen in Lapland until some few decades ago. His antagonist is shooting arrows at him. The third person holds nothing, but is seen in the act of dancing and bears an extraordinary resemblance to the cele- brated figure of a sorcerer or wizard depicted in the Pyrenean cave Les Trois Frères. Here is proof beyond question of a cultural and artistic affinity between the hunters (or breeders?) of Lake Ladoga, who later spread to the shores of the White Sea by way of what is now Karelia – and the reindeer- hunters of a far more southerly land who flourished in the great age of the Upper Palæolithic.

Figs. 7, 8
Fig. 7

Fig. 8
Fig. 9

The great innovation of the period was without doubt the use of the ski, of which ample traces are still to be seen in the cave-drawings of this same zone as well as of northern Scan- dinavia. The ski stood for an epoch in which hunting on a big scale was followed by the domestication of the hunted herds.

Fig. 10

It has been maintained that a considerable hiatus occurs between remains discovered on the shores of the North Sea, and any earlier traces of these hunters, who moved in this direction when they left the marshy zones of Lake Onega and Lake Ladoga. But if we examine, for example, a rock-drawing discovered at Ruändan, in the Swedish district of Mittådalen, in which a group of elk and reindeer is portrayed, we see that stylistically it is endowed with practically the same spirit of schematic pictorialism as appears at Zalavrouga – and also on the sacred drums of the Lappish shamans. All these artistic manifestations may be dated back to 2000 B.C. Other natural-

Plate I

Fig. 11

Fig. 10. Prehistoric skier; graffiti in rock discovered at Rödöy, Tjötta, North Norway

istic pictures from recent times in southern Scandinavian regions would appear to be linked more closely in spirit with a a more archaic culture. They are in fact characterized by a striking approach to the Magdalenian pictorial-type. Could it be, then, that prehistoric Sweden offers us the evidence of two separate epochs and cultures?

The Swede Gustaf Hallström, in the course of his archae-ological research in Lapland, came upon some ancient utensils going back to the Stone Age. On the score of their workmanship and fashioning, he classified them as of 'Nordic' origin.[3] Hallström then formulated the theory that during the climatic change which coincided in Scandinavia with the dawn of the Iron Age (known in the Edda as *Fimbulvinter*) the Lapps were still migrating from Finland towards Norr-land: their contact with Nordic populations did not therefore take place till a comparatively late date. Here is a hypothesis which would appear to be borne out by the linguistic theory of K. B. Wiklund. According to this, the Lapps first came into contact with the peoples of the north seven, or perhaps five, centuries before our era. The evidence is adduced from studying the German origin of some Lappish words. Wiklund, how-ever, believed that the Lapps had already been in the north for some time, and that it was the Germanic tribes who migrated from the south at this period. After the clash, the Lapps (still according to this hypothesis) decided to turn back southwards themselves. Why they thus decided to retrace their steps is not

Fig. 11. Reindeer-group from a rock-drawing at Zalavrouga, on the White Sea, USSR

clear. But all the evidence points to the fact that their decision had something to do with the climatic change referred to by Hallström. Lower temperatures once again caused an influx of herds of wild reindeer into the southern zones and those who lived by the reindeer were therefore forced back along with them.

There was a time when it was generally agreed that the Lapps stemmed from Central Russia even if the exact district of their origin could not be pinned down. Then, about 1920, Komsa became a name to conjure with for all who took an interest in this mysterious people.

Komsa is the name of a Norwegian district on the coast of the North Sea, and one which has come in for special study on the part of Anders Nummedal. It has yielded finds of tools and other objects which have proved to be of Palæolithic workman-ship. The prehistoric site needed no excavation. Once it had been close to the sea. The method of working the stone (quartz) and the types of objects produced are not easy to define. An affinity seems to be established with the South-Central European Mousterian, and this is especially apparent in the workmanship of the knives. But it might equally be held that all these artifacts continue the tradition of the better Aurignacian craftsmen; scrapers, chisels, as well as the form of arrowhead, provide a valid argument for this view. But the Mousterian and Aurignacian periods, at any rate in South-Central Europe, belong to the last phase of the Ice Age, when the ice was expanding southwards, while these finds at Komsa are attributable to the period of the last ice-recession in the Norwegian record. Moreover, when we consider that the same traditions of work have also turned up in Poland, at depths corresponding to Late Magdalenian, the style becomes still more difficult to classify. How was it possible for an unknown people, then living on the margins of the last tracts of melting ice, to be still in possession of the elements of so ancient a culture? Can it be that these 'Magdalenian' relics of Komsa prove that a hunting-people could, after a long migration, still maintain ties with the culture of a past age? We may wonder if we are here in contact with one branch of a people which for a time was also scattered over the plains of France, right down to the Pyrenees.

Could the reindeer have been followed from so far south right up to the wintry coasts of Norway? Many scholars considered this to be unlikely.

But a few – among them, Pia Lavosa Zambotti,[4] – while leaving aside the Lappish question proper, did arrive at the conclusion that 'in the Late Magdalenian period, in France, in Belgium, as throughout northern and central Germany, one finds a second *floruit* of the style characteristic of the Final Aurignacian as exemplified in Poland and neighbouring regions'. This opinion is also supported by the fact that in Norway, through the whole of the Neolithic Age, we find a culture which evokes the technically better tradition of the ice-recession period.

The discoveries made at Komsa provided a good many new problems, not a few of them of a somewhat contradictory nature.

Ernst Manker, who in addition to making a profound study of the Lapps, has also conducted countless expeditions and reconnaissances among the mountains forming the watershed between Norway and Sweden, sees some similarity between the Komsa finds and the discoveries made in the course of excavations at Varberg on the west coast of Sweden. He makes the assertion[5] that in both these zones we have encountered traces of a Brachycephalic people of small stature; and his investigations into the origins of the reindeer-herding culture convince him that definite links exist between the Lappish culture and the eastern culture of the White Sea region (Zalavrouga) and the Urals (Ostyak). His conclusion, though he stops short of stating it categorically, would appear to be that an archaic Lappish culture was widespread while as yet the Lapps had not actually set foot in Scandinavia; that is to say, Manker does not believe Lapps to have been responsible for these Komsa artifacts.[6]

Some authorities have suggested that Komsa was a temporary refuge from severe climatic conditions where the inhabitants 'over-wintered'. K. B. Wiklund is the founder of this school of thought, and those who share his view claim that during the last period of the Ice Age, there were regions of Norway where it was quite possible for human life to survive. Wiklund avers that the Lapps, the remnant of the racial progenitors of both Mongols and Europeans, had been cut off from their kinsfolk by some huge natural catastrophe. This is the significance Wiklund attaches to Komsa. For him, Komsa commemorates a group of Palæo-Lapps who, finding it impossible to live with the ice all round them, took up 'winter quarters' in some propitious spot on the North Sea coast, and survived – thereby offering a human parallel to the zoological example of the lemming, the little rodent of the north which is capable of migration on such a formidable scale. When the ice had disappeared, these Palæo-Lapps moved off east and south, encountering fresh peoples.[7]

Others claim that the culture exemplified at Komsa was not indigenous. They accept as proven Wiklund's 'over-wintering' theory but they believe that the people responsible for these artifacts came from the east by way of Karelia. Anathon Björn[8] held this view, which happily did not conflict with the prevalent hypothesis of a Lappish migration from the Russian plains as a consequence of the glaciation. Only Wiklund and a few others adhered to the theory of 'over-wintering' of pro-longed duration, on the North Sea coast. Wiklund's study of this problem, which called for a vast amount of research, was interrupted by his untimely death in 1934.

Our most important problem remains that of putting a date to the first settlement of the Palæo-Lapps in Scandinavia.

Wiklund and Tanner, authors of a very fine book on the Skolt groups,[9] had a name for the Komsa people. They called them 'Archæo-Lapps' or 'Ur-Lapps'. Other scholars have given them different names, but almost all were in agreement that they belonged to a Palæo-Arctic people whose latest descendants are the Lapps we know today.

A theory has recently been formulated by Gutorm Gjessing,[10] the Norwegian archaeologist. From recent archae-ological discoveries which he has described in a number of works, Gjessing deduces that these Palæo-Lapps belonged to an Arctic-littoral cultural cycle which covered a greater area than had any previous culture. But he also admits the striking resemblance between the cultural style typified by the Komsa discoveries and that to be seen much farther south. He has established a relationship between discoveries made in Russia, Poland and France, and the objects which have come to light on the Norwegian coast. In all these he sees an extraordinary evidence of Lapponoid characteristics; very often, again, objects unearthed in Lapland show unmistakable signs of a culture with a southern, and an eastern, tinge. Briefly,

Gjessing's view is that external influences in Arctic-Scandinavian culture were of the widest variety, being drawn from all regions bordering on the Arctic Circle, and not those of Europe alone.

We might classify this culture as the 'sub-glacial tundra type', This would conform with Gjessing's view as to the inter-relationship of various cultures and would take into account the ethnological contributory forces of other Arctic peoples.

The second millennium before our era can perhaps safely be given as a date for the incursion of the reindeer-hunters into Scandinavia. This supposition is based on an historical fact: this was the era in which many of the hunting-peoples left Karelia. In the third millennium B.C. a formidable wave of peoples, whose tongue was Indo-European, descended upon the Baltic regions, upsetting the existence of many tribes who had made their home in those immense forests, and forcing them to leave their ancient hunting-grounds and the lakes and rivers where they had found the fishing so profitable. In order to escape from these ferocious newcomers and their spears, the uprooted tribes scattered in all directions; those whose homeland lay on the fringe of the great wooded belt forming a half-circle round the Baltic shores fled towards what is now Finland, where they encountered groups of the ancient reindeer-hunters. It is a matter of controversy whether the newcomers subjugated these groups or whether they only drove the mass of them into more northerly regions – already doubtless familiar to many of them as hunting-grounds during the less rigorous seasons of the year. All this happened some 5,000 years ago and traces of this migration, which tended farther and farther north, have been discovered in Finland and along the Gulf of Bothnia. At the same time the lichen was beginning to acclimatize itself, and this was a contributing factor behind the great trek of the reindeer-hunters.

Among the tribes displaced by the warriors with their spears, who were none other than the ancient Germani, there were some Finnish peoples; but, according to recent scholars who make this claim, they appeared in Finland only 2,500 years ago, having first made a long sojourn in the region which constitutes the so-called Baltic countries of today – Esthonia, Latvia and Lithuania. Now, there is scientific proof that at this same period, Lapps were to be found in the northernmost zones of Scandinavia. It is clear therefore that the Lapps occupied, in all, a wide territory, taking in the regions between the lakes Ladoga and Onega and the White Sea; the Kola peninsula; Finland and northern Scandinavia.

Some groups of Lapps appear to have inhabited the LadogaOnega district within historical times, so that there are some grounds for the assertion, made in a few quarters, that a number of them were brought under Finnish dominion, although the great majority enjoyed the freedom of the north, with all the hunting and fishing the north provided. There is an ancient legend among the Lapps which might well be brought up in support of this suggested chapter of their history. In olden times, we learn, the Lapps had to submit to the assaults of an enemy tribe. For many long years they were its subjects, and from it they learned the tongue which thenceforward they spoke. This predatory race the Lapps called Cutte or Chudes, and they preserve a lively enough record of their captors. The fact that now, in modern times, the Lapps speak a FinnoUgrian language, while in earlier days they certainly had a tongue of their own, lends some substance to the story. For a very long period, it would seem, they lived in subjection to Finnish tribes, and the new language was gradually imposed on the whole people.

At the same time, it is also claimed nowadays, and on good authority, that Lappish as spoken is a more ancient language than Finnish, although it belongs to the same language group.

CHAPTER II

The Earliest Historical Records

THE FIRST MENTION of the people of the north to have come down to us is that by the Roman historian, Publius Cornelius Tacitus. In his *Germania,* after describing the life and customs of the 'barbarian' tribes inhabiting the very fringe of the world, so far as it was then known, he goes on to speak of a people he calls the Fenni,[11] of whom he. writes: 'They are extraordinarily wild and horribly poor. They have no arms, no horses, no permanent homes. They live on grass, they dress in skins, they sleep on the ground. They pin their one hope to the arrow. Lacking iron, they use bone to provide it with a sharp point. Their hunting provides food for men and women alike; the womenfolk, in fact, follow the men everywhere and demand their share of the prey. The children have no other protection from storm and tempest than may be granted them by a few interwoven branches. In such a refuge, the young gather, and the old retire to it. Yet it is this people's belief that in some manner they are happier than those who sweat out their lives in the field and wear out their strength in houses, trafficking with their own fortune and that of others. Careless towards both men and gods, they have achieved the most difficult thing of all: they have ceased to feel the harrying of men's desires.'

This page of Tacitus shows the manners and customs of the Finns as differing very little from those which, in that era, must have characterized the Lapps too – to which, indeed, they still cling. In point of fact, nearly all authorities have identified these Fenni with the Lapps.

It is worth bearing in mind that Tacitus was writing this about A.D. 98, by which time, as we have already seen, Lapp groups had been long established in Scandinavia—this is amply supported by recent archaeological excavations. Yet

Tacitus makes no reference to great herds of reindeer, from which the hunting-people could never have been far removed. But his statement that the Fenni lived on grass is only another way of saying that they depended on hunting for their food. Some writers seven or eight centuries later make no mention of the reindeer either. From all this we may assume that these animals, in Tacitus's day, covered far more southerly territories than is nowadays the case. The explanation may well be that as they were as common as other horned animals there was nothing special about them to record.

So far as the name 'Fenni' is concerned, Manker draws our attention[12] to the fact that we have here nothing less than an ancient Nordic word *finnar* or *finner* – meaning Lapps. He reminds us that the root may still be seen in the Norwegian regional name 'Finnmark' – that is, 'land of the Lapps'. The Finnish-speaking population, on the other hand, went by the name of Kväner until they assumed that of a single tribe, Suomi. When Manker speaks of a 'Nordic' word, he refers to the language of the Germanic-speaking Scandinavian people. There is a hint here that Tacitus knew his Fenni by hearsay – the hearsay of Germanic Scandinavians. Word of them must have come from Germanic tribes beyond the Baltic, seeing that, to our knowledge, Tacitus never set foot in Scandinavia.

In Roman history, the 'Fenni' were the inhabitants of the north-eastern zones of the great Germanic plains: indeed, at one point (*Germania,* XLVI, 1) Tacitus pleads ignorance as to whether the Peucini, the Venedi and the Fenni are numbered among the Germani or the Sarmati; from which it is clear that not only did the Fenni live to the east of the Germani, they were also likely to be confused with the non-Germanic peoples scattered between the Carpathians and the Russian plain and labelled 'Sarmati' by our historian. There is one passage in Tacitus whose vital importance everyone has overlooked. In Chapter XLVI of the *Germania* he gives a somewhat diffuse account of the customs of the Suioni, placing these Germanic peoples in southern Scandinavia. According to him, they live surrounded by the sea; for he is writing at a time when the Gulf of Bothnia was thought to be connected with the Arctic Ocean, making Norway and Sweden an island. Tacitus opens Chapter XLVII with a description of how the land of the Suioni comes to an end at another sea, 'where the Sun, though already setting, casts a light of such strength that it continues even until dawn with sufficient power to obscure the stars'. Here is ample evidence that Tacitus was well-informed. The phenomenon he is describing is the 'midnight sun', and in that latitude of the Arctic Circle it has indeed a duration of two months. At the close of Chapter XLVI, again, Tacitus remarks, 'Beyond the Suioni are to be found the tribes of the Sitoni. Of similar manners and customs, they differ in one particular: they are commanded by a woman, so deep have they plumbed the depths not alone of a lost freedom but of servitude itself.'

This passing reference made by Tacitus to the fact of the Sitoni being governed by a woman could easily be ascribed to legend were we not aware of the special importance of the woman in the Lapp family group. This is not the place to go into the ancient rites practised in the celebrations of *Māddâr-akko* – Woman the Creator; but it is worth mentioning that not only did the women hunt with the menfolk, but there were times when particularly skilled women led the hunt. So much can be proved. It is also relevant to recall that there are elements in Lapp culture which appear to indicate a matri-archal society.

Now, if the word *finner* was a genuine Nordic or Scandina-vian word, it could most appropriately have been applied to the Sitoni rather than to the Fenni-inhabitants of the Sarmatian plain. And Tacitus could never have had in mind, while writing his history, anything on the lines of the eventual migrations and possible merging of the two peoples: for all he knew, they were separated by the Gulf of Bothnia, which made Sweden into an island. Is it beyond the bounds of possibility that the Germanic peoples of the well-wooded Ercinia and Vistula regions understood by Fenni the inhabitants of terri-tories to the east of their own – while the same name, if we are to believe the students of Norse, was used by the ancient colonizers of Sweden to indicate the Lapps?

Within historic times, as we know, a rearguard of Lapps remained between Lake Ladoga and Lake Onega. Does Tacitus mean these? If he does, he is providing the one possible justification for our recognition of the ancient hunters in the Fenni of the *Germania*. On the other hand, there is nothing to stop us from coming to a very different conclusion – that the name Fenni bears no reference to the Lapps and that writers succeeding Tacitus have only perpetuated an error in thinking it ever bore one.

Was not the name Finnmark, then, given to the region to designate a land of the Lapps – Fenni? Everything points to this, since the true Finns were known by other names. All record of the Sitoni has disappeared, along with the name itself. Yet there they were, Tacitus tells us, living in northern Scandinavia within historic times.

Historians and monks now devised a special name for the Lapps. They call them *Scritifinni* – that is 'Finni sciatori' – following Tacitus, whose 'Fenni' they took to be the Lapps.

For four centuries following Tacitus we have no mention of the Lapps, though it is known today that they were at that period scattered over the regions to the north of the Gulf of Bothnia, along the valleys of the Swedish and Norwegian mountains spilling into what is now Dalecarlia (Dalarna), which marked their most westerly penetration.

During these four centuries, too, they came into ever closer contact with the agricultural populations living in the more southerly part of the country. But in these early days of the Christian Era, nobody took any interest in the Lapps. Interest was centred on other parts of Europe: this was the eventful time when the Roman Empire was coming to an end and a new dominion of barbarians into being.

The only writer of those times, or anywhere near them, who so much as mentions the peoples beyond the Baltic – and his account is merely based on scraps of information from travellers and merchants – was Procopius (A.D. 490–562), the famous historian of the Goths.[13] Describing their land and their mode of life, in about 550, he tells us of a Nordic people of non-Germanic race called 'Scritifinni' – nomads devoted to hunting and fishing, living in cabins of earth-clods and interwoven branches. Procopius felt a great revulsion for this barbarous people, and he gives a picture of them which could not be more down-to-earth in tone. He tells us flatly that of all the races living in 'far Thule', the 'Scritifinni' alone adopt 'the ways of the beasts'. When he says that they possessed neither clothes nor shoes, Procopius of course means clothes and shoes as they were understood by the Germani. He must have seen or heard tell of these men and women draped in animal skins from head to foot. What a rude awakening for a man of refinement! A man accustomed to the pomp and circumstance of the Byzantine court!

Procopius was further horrified by the fact that these savages neither cultivated the land nor knew the sweetening influence of the vine, but, men and women alike, indulged in one wild relentless welter of hunting, to keep body and soul together. The country, our historian proceeds, 'is thick with vast, frozen forest and ridged by mountains teeming with wild life', the latter a godsend to a people dependent on animals for food and clothing. But to turn a thick stiff fur into a passable outfit is no easy matter; these barbarians, lacking even the needle to sew with, just draped over their shoulders a mass of skins held together with the dead animals' sinews! Procopius gives us an outrageously exaggerated picture of what was actually an ancient custom among these nomadic Lappish tribes when he laments their total ignorance of civilized child-rearing. Lapp mothers, he informs us, do not breast-feed their young. They wrap them in some skin, hang them up in a tree, give them a marrow-bone to suck – and off they go, hunting with their husbands. The truth is soberer. Procopius has embroidered the plain fact that the mothers do sometimes hang the cradle to a branch, if they have to go off for a very short time.

Fig. 12. Prehistoric ski, dated at 1500 B.C. discovered in a marsh near Lomsjökullen, Sweden. Now in the Nordiska Museum, Stockholm

But the most interesting note is struck by those who seek to see the Lapps in those 'Fenni' of Tacitus. In explaining Procopius's new name for them, they point out that he has taken the ancient Nordic 'Fenni' and coupled it with another word of equally ancient Scandinavian origin whose meaning we now know – the modern Swedish equivalent being *skrida*. How dumbfounded the Swedish people must have been when they saw these hunters of the north fix two thin little boards to their feet and go slipping with the utmost ease over the snow! It is understandable that this, the Lapps' most striking characteristic, should be the one signalled out when they were given a nickname.

We know that the ski-stick found at Kalvträsk has been dated back, by pollen-analysis, to 2000 B.C., while Lapp skis have come to light whose origin can be ascribed beyond all doubt to the period between 1500 and 1000 B.C. In 1945, in

marshy country near Lomsjökullen, ten kilometers north of
Vilhelmina in Sweden, a ski was found which experts pro-
nounced to be definitely of Lappish type. Those who support
the theory of the identity between Fenni and Lapps affirm that
the *Scritifinni* mentioned by Procopius were highly-skilled
skiers, such as the Lapps have always been. It did not occur to
them that a scientific method would one day be able to put a
date to the Lappish skis which have come to light, and that
that date would carry us back to an epoch which ante-dates
Tacitus by as long as our own post-dates him.

Fig. 12

Plate 4

And here is Francesco Negri, in the seventeenth century,
interpreting the newfangled name which Procopius had
devised:

'As for this name Skrifinni, in my belief it fits these same
Lapps, who have been so variously styled by various writers.
For the difference is but a small one between Skrifinni and
Skierfinni, that is, the Finni of the Skier, for with their *skier*
they run swiftly. Again, there is but little difference between
Skrifinni and Skritofinni, which is to say Finni that are
archers . . .14'

One writer of the sixth century, Jordanes, who belonged to a
noble Gothic family, speaks of a people he calls the Screre-
finni,15 whose territory stretched from the Gulf of Bothnia to
the central regions of Sweden and Norway. Here they came to
a great extent under Gothic influence, thus gathering some
notion of the runic alphabet brought from the Black Sea.
Traces of this – and the point is of the utmost importance to
the student of Scandinavian history and the Viking expeditions – were noted among the Lapps by the missionary Knud
Leem. In 1725 he recognized runes in certain designs executed
by the Lapps on the magic drums of their shamans.

In 780 Paulus Diaconus, the Lombard monk, better
known under the name of Varnefrid, gave us the first accurate description of a people he calls (writing in Latin)

Scritobini.[16] Paulus relates how they lived in 'the other part of Germania', that is, beyond the Baltic, in a land white with snow even during the summer months. According to this monk, here was a people who lived off the wild beasts, eating the flesh and clothing themselves in the skins. Their name, he records, derived from a certain word in their tongue which meant 'to run' – for 'slipping along on two pieces of curved wood, they were able to outpace the wild animals'. But what name Paulus had in mind is not clear; he only tells us that it forms part of the 'barbarous tongue'. Resorting to the language of the Lapps, we find ourselves thinking of the word *sabme*. In all Lappish dialects this signifies the people's racial name.

But if we assume Paulus to have meant the word 'Scritobini', then we already know its etymology. Yet this would be a case of what might be called 'scientific' nomenclature – in the sense that the name was created by historians, artificially.

Further on in this Lombard monk's description we come across this statement: 'where these people dwell there is an animal which recalls the deer'. Is he implying that the rein-deer – certainly a member of the deer family – was already domesticated by the Lapps? It should be noted, however, that the phrase quoted follows the monk's description of how the Lapps used skis to catch wild beasts. This suggests that the Lapps in those days may have kept reindeer in their home-steads in order to milk them, or more probably as decoys for the other wild beasts, while continuing to hunt, on skis, the great herds which were still at liberty among the mountains.

Vague and inconclusive references crop up from time to time in ancient sagas and Norse legend – handed down from Norwegians, Icelanders and Vikings – to the presence of these nomads on the Atlantic coasts. Did they establish themselves there? A Viking influence is certainly to be noted in the artistic motifs executed by the hunters on their buckles, belts, utensils, their coloured sashes, and, above all, on their skis.

Figs. 13, 14

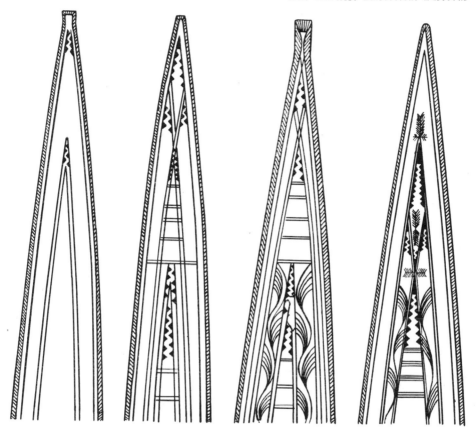

Fig. 13. Four Lappish skis (the forward ends shown) ornamented in Viking style, from Mola, in Lycksele, Sweden

But the Vikings, that proud, violent people thirsting for adventure, left their country in large numbers. Some went to Iceland, others to Greenland whence, like Leif Eirikson, seeking new landfalls in the south, they discovered America unawares. Others, thenceforward to be known as Normans, set out for Europe's temperate zones and settled there.

The Lapps would appear to have been the solitary inhabitants of the great tundra lands which start from the Atlantic fjords, cross the highlands of Finnmark and decline into the boundless plains of Finland. The bold seafarers of the blond hair and the glistening helmets decked out with horns or

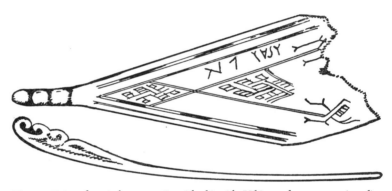

Fig. 14. Point of a ninth-century Lappish ski with Viking-style ornamentation, discovered in marshy ground at Ajaur, in Lycksele, North Sweden

crow's wings had by now left for distant lands. The Svear and other races cultivated the milder stretches washed by the Baltic. The Finnish Suomi and their tribesmen had settled once and for all among vast conifer forests and lakes.

Towards the close of the ninth century, a Norwegian called Othere, a viceroy as we might call him of the Håloga district, was commanded by his sovereign Harald to pay an official visit to King Alfred of England. Alfred at this time was at the zenith of his achievements. After his victory over Guthrun and the Danes, he was devoting himself to the translation of famous works which he hoped to spread among his rude and uninstructed people. When Othere began to describe his own land (the Tromsö region of today) and the little men who lived in the north, the King of England, all enthusiasm, demanded full details. And when he came to translate the seven books which constitute the historical work *Adversus Paganos* by the Spanish priest Orosius, he wished to make certain modifica-tions in the accounts given of the northern peoples, then so little known. Thus it came about that Alfred tells us of the *Scridefinnas* and of Othere, who had 'six hundred tame deer called *rhanas*'. Six of these Othere used as a 'decoy', or a lure, with his eye on the untamed herds still roaming the mountain-sides.

In this connection, Manker[17] is of the opinion that Othere's herds were tended and followed throughout the migrations by Lappish herdsmen, who must therefore have been prepared to offer their service to foreigners. But it must be admitted that Othere's claim to a herd six hundred strong may have been no more than bragging – a wish to magnify his importance in King Alfred's eyes.

Be that as it may, this document of King Alfred's is surely the first in which the Saxon name for the animal appears – *rhana,* originally pronounced, according to some linguistic students, with an aspirated *h*. It has been held in some quarters that *rhana* – or *hrana* – is of the same origin as the word for 'run' – *rennan* – still to be seen in some form in several Anglo-Saxon derivatives. This root-word now came to designate the reindeer of the Germanic lands. The Lapps' own name for the animal was *boazo*. Then again, in Lappish the species is known as *sarves* (mainly applied to the male), with the feminine *vāžâ*.

My own opinion is that the interpretation above is on the inconclusive side. Surprisingly, in ancient Basque (a non-Indo-European tongue) the word for reindeer is *orena*. An aspirated *h* here seems to have become an *o*. This assumes particular interest if we recall the studies made by a Basque author, Telesforo De Aranzadi, who claimed to have lighted upon cultural and anthropological links between the Lapps and the Basques. Let us recall too that some eastern Siberian peoples (the Orokhi) take their name from the Mansk word for reindeer, *oro*.

CHAPTER III

Missionaries and Merchants Discover
a Peace-Loving People

RIGHT UP TO THE TIME of the Danish monk Saxo Gram-maticus – about 1200 – a virtual silence reigns concerning the activities of our barbarian hunters. It is broken only by a fleeting mention of them in 1060 on the part of Adam of Bremen. This writer, after his travels in the Jutland Peninsula, did refer in his account to the 'Scridfinni'. Not that he says anything of importance. Of all the aspects of this rude race, the only one he thought worth mentioning was their ability to run on skis.

Saxo Grammaticus, on the other hand, supplies us for the very first time with the name *Lappia.* He uses it to designate 'the uninhabitable region wherein dwell the Scridfinni, hunters armed with arrows and spear, swiftly running on pieces of wooden board and much given to magic.'[18] Here for the first time, too, we hear of the tents the nomads carry on their migra-tions, loading their reindeer with stakes, poles and skins.

If we look at the Finnish etymology of the word *Lappia,* we find that Saxo meant to identify the land of the Scridfinni with the very desert-fringe of Europe. Gradually, Finni and Scridfinni, under their various spellings, yielded to Lappi. We find it here and there in very early print, for example in some of the tales of Claudius Clavus and Michel Beheim. But popular fantasy supplied other names – sometimes the oddest – for the northern people, all unbeknown to them of course. Some of these names are quite incomprehensible. A glance at such old, forgotten texts as were published will give us 'Himantopi', 'Cinocefali', 'Biarmi' – the last one admittedly containing a clear hint at a country of bears, if we trace it back to Swedish. In the Middle Ages, the Lapps themselves had equally far-fetched notions: that they had only one leg, like the fantastic Unipedi of Vinland the Good discovered in some vague America by the Vikings; or one eye, in the middle of the brow, like Polyphemus of old. And amazing as it may seem, Manker, as recently as 1945, transcribed a legend told him by some Lapps in the village of Tuorpon, in which the Poly-phemus-myth is applied to an ancient character in Lappish mythology.[19] Others, again, thought that the little men of the north were none other than the descendants of those gnomes with which Germanic folklore peopled the deep forest of Central Europe. For a long while, there were many who identified them with the Ulda – pure sprites of Nordic legend. The outside world was beginning to take an interest in them. No longer were they to be allowed to remain an unknown quantity in their boundless mountain solitude.

The year 1546 saw the death of Martin Luther. His disciples speedily took up the task of spreading the Gospel to those races still living in the shadow of ancient pagan cults. In North-Central Europe, a religious renaissance was in the air. Lutheran pastors hastened north, where the greatest numbers had yet to be brought into the fold. Already between the ninth century and the twelfth, Christianity had been promulgated in Scandinavia, but it was not until the sixteenth that the Lutheran doctrine, fresh from its conquest of the Germanic world, reached the tundra and the mountains where an ancient race of men lived in company with the gentlest of the animals.

In 1555 a book was published in Rome under the title *Historia de Gentibus Septentrionalibus* by Olaus Magnus[20] the exiled Roman Catholic Archbishop of Uppsala. He and his brother both made important contributions to our knowledge of the geography of the north in the sixteenth century, and this work in particular provides us with a useful picture of life in Scandinavia, although the information about the Lapps is rather less reliable than that relating to the peasant population.

The Lapps certainly have their place in his *Historia*. This learned work has its authentic side, for it records the actual first-hand findings of missionaries working in the northern field, and of fur-traders too. But there is the same admixture of the fantastic; the author could not keep out the stubborn inventions of popular fancy. Oral tradition and Norse sagas combine with fact to form a bewildering kaleidoscope. Here are the old stories resuscitated – people with one eye, burrowing underground for the winter, and hibernating like bears and dormice. Other travellers had the Lapps living in tree-tops – the trees growing to immense height on the very edge of the known world, and from such eyries contemplating the thunderous ice-tides of the ultimate sea.

Fig. 15. Njâllâ or storehouse for food, painted on a Lappish drum

The whole farrago stemmed from sober fact, the sober fact of a hundred little items of exact information. Unfortunately, as often happens, in passing from one pair of lips to the next, they became more and more distorted. For instance, in winter the Lapps do indeed construct cabins which are half underground; they hold the heat better. The Lapps did indeed use the tree-tops – in so far as they mounted their store-houses on stakes to protect their meat from the depredations of hungry wolves and wolverines.

Fig. 15
Plate 21

Olaus, however, does give a factually exact description of ski-ing. We learn that not only were the Lapps capable of covering wide tracts of snow at high speed, but they could execute the most complicated manœuvres on steep slopes whenever the fancy took them, using a stick to assist their movements. Olaus is also the first to give us any description of their boats: these they constructed by joining together pieces of wood with reindeer sinews. Modern explorers have found a few traces of such primitive craft. And we gather from Olaus that even in those distant days some groups of Lapps paid a form of tax – as Othere had implied to King Alfred – to certain privileged interests to which they consigned large numbers of furs. Naturally the practice was subject to abuses and the so-called 'Lapp-sheriff', who should have looked into the question of these payments, was often powerless to act. This system of taxation for the wretched Lapps was soon to be abolished in the reign of Karl IX, the son of Gustavus Vasa.

Fig. 16. Lapp skier armed with a cross-bow, in a seventeenth-century engraving

But something absolutely new was happening in the frozen seas that washed the north coasts of Scandinavia. In 1553 an English expedition left home waters to brave the rigours and perils of Arctic navigation. Sir Hugh Willoughby, in search of the north-eastern passage to the Orient, touched at the shores of what was Russian Lapland with his two ships 'Hope' and

'Confidence'. A third, 'Edward Bonaventure', after losing all contact with the other two in a severe storm, sailed up the Dvina. Sir Hugh went ashore in the hope of finding food and comforts, but the men were in very poor shape. They were no match for the intense cold and the storm-winds that beat down on those desolate lands.

In the spring of the following year, their frozen, huddled bodies were discovered by Lappish hunters. The leader of the expedition was found still seated, as he had died, in a rough shanty he had contrived out of a few pieces of wood, with his log still before him.

The missionaries, however, did not give up. Some of them, pushing farther and farther north along the Norwegian fjords, came upon hunters and their families performing rites and sacrifices of which all trace is lost. But they were unable to remain in contact with such Lapps. The time came when the latter, being nomads, set off inland, into a frozen desert.

It was at this period that one traveller, exploring the banks of the River Torne, north of the Arctic Circle, visited the encampments of Tingvara and Siggevara, which were among the most ancient known in Swedish Lapland. In fact the zone was mapped, somewhat approximately it is true, by Oluff Tresk in 1543. His map shows that at one point on the river there existed a trading post, and we are told that it had got well under way. The first merchants exchanged goods with the Lapps on the barter system. A place was decided upon for the Lapps to leave their skins and reindeer-horn. Then, in hiding, they would wait for the merchants to come, bringing with them their own goods. The exchange proceeded without the two parties seeing each other.

In 1570, sixty charts of the north were made by one Franz Hogenburg from the designs of Abraham Ortelius, the Antwerp cartographer. With their great topographical detail, they came as a revelation to students of the period. Of special

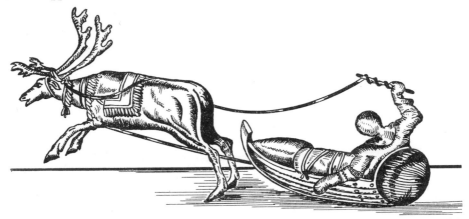

Fig. 17. Seventeenth-century engraving showing a sled drawn by a reindeer. The typical canoe-shape of the sled is clearly visible. The trace passes between the animal's legs

interest is the fact that Ortelius divided the upper reaches of Scandinavia into three regions: the area up in the north, towards the Arctic, he called Scricfinnia. To the centre and towards the east – the zones today belonging to Finland and the USSR – he gave the name of Lappia. The western region he called Finmarchia.

Ortelius, in 1554, had attended the Frankfurt Fair. This saw a gathering of merchants and travellers from all over Europe, and here he had met the Flemish geographer Gerard Kremer – the 'Mercator' who in the same year had completed his work on a map of Europe. How much these two geographers must have had to talk about! Finding themselves in agreement over questions which, in those days of momentous discoveries, divided the entire world, they decided to travel together. And they must have asked a host of questions of everyone who had come from afar to Frankfurt, for it could scarcely have been lost on these two that when it comes to knowing a country, there is no one like a merchant.

Mercator's northern Scandinavia of 1554 was given only two names – the old Nordic names of Finmarchia and Lappia.

The latter comprises the Kola peninsula and the region round Lake Inari. While this artificial division stubbornly persisted, the country did begin to assume some accurate topographical detail on the map.

Merchants from the northern countries set out for Lapland by all the means of transport then available to them: on horseback and by boat. Disembarking at Luleå, they sought out the nomads and their furs. With the conquest of the Free City of Novgorod by the Voivod of Moscow, the Novgorod merchants no longer enjoyed the isolated splendour of a commercial monopoly along the northern coast-line. Russia stepped in, sending her own bargainers along the Murmansk seaboard and the Gulf of Kandalaksa. Now, it can be said, the discovery of the Lapps really began. A new world, whose existence Europe had never suspected, was suddenly revealed to these voyagers. A window had been opened upon an ancient past. But nothing in that ancient world was dead, nothing had

Fig. 18. Seventeenth-century engraving of a Lapp hunter with a large bow of Asiatic type. His wife carries a bark cradle slung across her shoulders

Fig. 19. Seventeenth-century engraving of a Lapp couple, the woman holding a cradled baby in her arms, the man carrying an axe

become fossilized with the passing of time. There was every sign of life and health. It was as if a prehistoric people had simply reappeared among the snows and marshes of the Arctic solitudes.

The famous Stroganoff family, who first opened up a route through the Urals allowing Russian expansion into Siberia, possessed by 1500 a monastery in the Kola peninsula. This was right inside Lappish territory. The monks' task was to convert the pagans. The Stroganoffs also possessed some establish-ments for the mining of salt, which was sold for Russian roubles. Commercialism and monastic affairs flourished side by side. But very soon, lured by rich minerals and abundant furs in Siberia, the Stroganoffs drew out of Lapland and left their bearded monks to their own devices. When the Stroganoffs went, the well-equipped warriors whose mission it had been to protect the monks from the 'savages' left too. Nevertheless the monks found that they were very well able to live and work without them. Giving offence to none, they continued their missionary work among a folk which was as harmless as themselves. For the Lapps were simple hunting-folk who, truth to tell, had always been baffled by the presence of so formidably accoutred a soldiery. Were the monks not there to preach the gospel of peace!

At the beginning of the seventeenth century, Lapland received a visit from the Commissary of King Charles IX of Sweden, Daniel Hjort. He did not fail to note that at one spot, where the River Torne broadens out between gentle hills, a large group of Lapps were to be found. The region they inhabited contained two lakes of striking beauty. It was the ideal situation for a church. Oluff Tresk had been on the right track; he had hit on the key-point of the whole district. At first a chapel was built on a tongue of land projecting south-east in the direction of the present Paksuniemi. Then by the command of a Royal Missive of 26 September 1673, a wooden church was built. From its little peninsula it dominates the river to this day.

In the meantime the parish priest of Piteå, Nicolas Andrae, had been coming into frequent contact with Lappish fur-traders along the Lule and Pite rivers. These hunters had come down from the highest mountains in Scandinavia, between Kebnekaise and Sulitelma. In the region encircled by these heights, verdant pasture-land alternated with perpetual ice. Wide lakes, brimful of fish, shimmered in the mountain air, and on their shores the Lapps had built earth cabins – at a distance of one day's march by the old paths. Very often, next to the hut there would be a *njâllâ* – the box, or miniature wooden shed, mounted on a pole, where the reindeer flesh was kept safe from wolves. Every lake had its little boat, hauled up on shore while out of use. From Lake Vastenjaure to the Great Lule Falls, from the ice of Blåmannsisen to the ancient battle-field of Jukkasjärvi, the Lapps had organized a chain of communication to maintain the bonds between the various *sii'dâ* – that is, between the family groups dotted here and there over so wide a territory – and to enable them to engage in their commerce. Here was a field for conversion, and its possibilities were not lost on the priest of Piteå. He made many attempts, not without some success. In 1619 he had a prayer-book printed in Lappish at Stockholm. This is the most ancient document we possess in the tongue of the nomads. A liberal contributor to the costs of publication was King Gustavus II Adolphus, providing the first official aid and encouragement the missionaries received.

One of their number, in the second half of the seventeenth century, was an Italian monk – certainly the first Italian to penetrate into Lapland – the priest Francesco Negri of Ravenna.

Scandinavian lore in Italy was a little hazy, even in these enlightened days. Not many years since, Norway and Sweden had still been thought to form an island – its northern half uninhabited.

The forty-year-old priest decided in 1663 to set out for these unknown lands, on what was to be a three-year journey. The reason for this he expressed in his *Viaggio Settentrionale*:[21] 'the whole glorious book of nature stood before him, and if he lacked the skill to read it, at least he wished to dedicate himself to one page . . . in order that he might observe therein the wondrous works of the Supreme Hand.'

He had already read the works of Olaus Magnus. His imagination was fired by many passages, though others left him somewhat unconvinced.

He crossed Germany and Poland, and journeyed on to Stockholm. Continuing overland, he came to the city of Torneå, which bestrides the present-day frontier between Sweden and Finland. He crossed the river and arrived at a mining-centre then known as Vappa-Vara – almost certainly the modern Svappavara. From this point onwards to the

North Cape – which he longed to reach as the ultimate northern limit of Europe, he was to face the greatest difficulties. After many a hardship, and a sojourn of many months in the heart of Lapland, he made his way back to Stockholm – still determined to reach his goal but by some more propitious route. A year went by. Then in October, at the onset of the terrible northern winter, he left Elsinore in Denmark. In the teeth of a storm he gained Bergen fjord, whence he set off once more, for Trondheim. From here, he made exploratory journeys which took him towards central Sweden – as far as the Östersund region. Back at Trondheim, he set out for the Lofoten Islands. Here, and along the Norwegian coast of Finnmark, right up to North Cape, he came upon many Lapps, whose way of life he describes in his own scholarly fashion. His 'Letters' caused more than one of the errors prevalent at the time to be rectified. They were published posthumously in Padua in the year 1700, and many readers profited by them. His writings are alive, and faithfully mirror what he saw with his own eyes. They make enjoyable reading and their literary excellence gives them a place in Italian seventeenth-century literature.

In 1673 a certain Johannes Schefferus[22] had brought out, in Frankfurt, a book called *Lapponia*. This followed hard on the heels of two works of kindred interest – Olaus Graan's *Relation om Lapparnas Ursprung* and Johannes Tornaeus's *Berättelse om Lapmarkerna och deras Tillstånd*. These were brief accounts of missionary work and exploration in Lapland, which were written (but not published) in 1672. Schefferus resorted freely to these two works to produce one of the best books ever written on the Lapps. It gave an accurate account of everything known about them and contained a mine of fresh information on the folklore, the customs and the religious rites of the people. If still more missionaries now made the journey to Lapland, it may well have been this book of Schefferus' that

E

Fig. 20. Engraving of a Lapp couple on a journey. The man is armed with a large bow and the woman leads a reindeer; a baby is carried in a cradle attached to the pack-saddle

spurred them on: here, for the very first time, was a genuine description of the country, detailed and sober.

And it was just at this period, memorable for such names as Tornaeus, Schefferus, Gabriel Tuderus, that serious speculation began about the origin of the Lapps. Early theories were re-formulated in terms of scientific plausibility. The nomadic hunters found themselves being slowly ringed round by a whole chain of new churches for their salvation. Their spires rose at Jukkasjärvi, Jokkmokk, Enontekis, Arvidsjaur, and Lycksele. At this last-named, the school of Skytte was founded. Named after its donor, it became a Lappish seminary.

This missionary zeal the Lapps found irksome. They retreated before it farther and farther into their mountains. Spring and autumn meant a pause, in 'camps', for the hunters – with the men from the south as neighbours. These the Lapps tried to avoid, but without success. The drums of the shamans, which Schefferus had described, fell silent. They disappeared into the forests with their drummers, the priests of the animistic cult. Deep in the forest, the old rites and sacrifices were furtively celebrated.

But before the end of the seventeenth century a special ordinance had been imposed on the Lapps. They must come to church, burying their drums and other religious symbols. But how many came? Only those brought along by force, one may be sure. The rest continued in hiding in their ancient retreats. Those who presented themselves to the pastor saw their drums piled up to make a crackling bonfire. Its flames were meant to extinguish ancient beliefs and superstitions, the racial memory of a people going back thousands of years.

In the depths of the forest, however, hidden drums still sounded. The Lapps were appealing to the Gods of the Tundra, the Gods of the Mountains, and of the Water, that they might grant them their help as they had done in the past. Again and again the shamans told their people that their gods had never deserted them. But the day came when some of their number were surprised and rounded up. And the old magicians who claimed the power to speak with the Spirits of the lakes and of the great rivers were burned alive – with their drums. This happened at Arjreplog in 1692.

In 1723 a new ruling was introduced. Every church must now have a school attached to it, for the purposes of religious instruction. A 'Lapp secretariat' was entrusted with this cultural charge.

Meanwhile, on the Atlantic coasts, the Lapps found themselves in complete possession, now that so many of the Vikings had gone. From the turn of the sixteenth century, the hunters and fishermen had been trading on a fair scale with the Baltic lands – later, with the port of Archangel. For a very long time, Russian merchants had been making the perilous voyage round North Cape, into the peaceful Norwegian fjords. The Lapps, on sighting their ships, would produce their mighty stocks of fur and reindeer-horn. Before long the Russians also came to appreciate the magnificent salmon and trout which their highly-skilled fisher-folk had taken from lake and river. Such barter kept them busy for many a long day – it continued right down the eighteenth century and went by the name of the 'Pomor Trade'.

Even before the fifteenth century drew to a close, the Norwegians had largely abandoned the fishing in their northern districts: the market had suffered a setback. But they had made considerable efforts to 'colonize' some of the less hilly regions along the fjords, which had the benefit of the Gulf Stream, and as a result the coast-dwelling Lapps were driven into high mountain country – forced to fall back on their winter quarters. A host of families who from time immemorial had lived by fishing now had to resort to hunting in order to survive.

Here, then, was an ancient group of fisher-folk chased away from the fringes of the civilized world into regions where an implacable winter reigned. It was to these exiles that a devout and deeply compassionate missionary, Knud Leem, brought new light and a new Word.

The year 1697 saw the birth of this man, who was destined to make such a magnificent contribution to the study, and the religious conversion, of these Norwegian Lapps. Knud Leem's father was a Bergen pastor. Following in his footsteps, the son studied theology in Copenhagen and in 1725, a fully qualified missionary, he was sent to the far north – the region known today as Finmark or Norwegian Lapland, but at that time a Danish possession. He made the journey by way of the Varanger peninsula, explored the Lakse fjord and met the inhabitants of Porsanger in order to convert them to the Faith. Here, Leem was at Europe's very last outpost – a tongue of land, utterly unknown, stretching out towards frozen seas, then the subject of as many wild tales as it had been in the time of Pytheas, the navigator of Marseilles. Tacitus himself averred that in this wild land, the traveller seemed to hear the sounds made by the Horses of the Sun. Leem had heard all these stories from boyhood, and he knew his Norse sagas. They must have been ringing in his ears as he set out. But when he reached the end of his journey, all he found was a people of hunters and fisher-folk living at peace in a world of silence and solitude.

Leem was given a warm welcome, and when he declared that he had been sent to bring the Word of a Man who had died in a distant land for the redemption of the human race, he was listened to with a great show of respect. Even so, the missionary realized that not all his listeners understood his message, and that his his first step must be to learn the language they spoke. He was very soon won over by the gentleness and the goodness of these men, grew to love them and resolved to dedicate his whole life to them.

Leem lived for a long time in Lappish cabins. His book[23] tells us of the rigours and discomforts he had to suffer. The cold was intense. Sleep and rest were all too brief. Nevertheless he bore it bravely enough, chiefly because he was so drawn towards the Lapps. Mild, gentle, eminently reasonable, they managed their lives without discord and in perfect tranquillity. Leem tells us that the herdsmen, in such free time as was left to them after they had tended their reindeer, would go out fishing on the lakes, in boats made of long, narrow, wooden boards joined together with fibre cording made from the roots of trees. Cormorants hunted the lakes as well as men, and the Lapps captured these great birds too, with the aid of a stick and a hook. The cormorants would swim along near the banks, with an eye on the water in search of fish, and so sometimes the Lapps would make a double catch: the cormorant, Leem points out, has a kind of sack under its beak in which it stores its prey, and this was often found full of fish when the bird was hooked.

Leem made scrupulously exact notes of everything that struck him. He found the Lapps were not, as they seemed to later travellers, of a Mongoloid type somatically. He noted the wide mouth, the black hair and olive skin, and the watery eyes – watery from the smoke in the tents and the dazzle of the snow. Many a time, when they came down from the mountains, following a reindeer herd, they would be snow-blind for a matter of days. The missionary amassed a great deal of information about these inhabitants of the far north, who were then almost unknown in Europe. His judgment is always trenchant, and at the same time understanding; it is far-reaching and loyal to the folk he served. How could it be otherwise, since he identified himself with a people of such fine calibre? At this period the Lapps were still almost entirely immune from the influences of western civilization. It is not surprising that Leem came to love these 'noble savages'.

On one occasion, when established in a village called Alten, Leem received a most welcome visit. A Lapp woman had made a long journey to wish him a happy Christmas. It was well into December, and the great plain and the mountains were covered with snow. Leem was taken aback to recognize his visitor as belonging to a *sii'dâ* some days journey from his village.

'I have come,' she said, 'because you told me to have faith. My baby was born, and all is well.'

Only then did the missionary recall that on leaving an encampment he had visited not long before, he had been accompanied for part of the way by a woman on the eve of child-birth and somewhat anxious over it. Now all her anxieties were over: she had been delivered five days before – only to make her way across a chain of all but impenetrable mountains, in terrible cold, to give the pastor her thanks.

It is Leem's opinion that such exceptional bodily vigour and powers of resistance partly the effect of consumption of fish-oil, on which the Lapps brought up their children from their earliest years.

Leem's account of the Lapps greatly increased the world's awareness of these northern people. Soon, priests, students, ethnographers, physicians, all types of men began to be attracted to the study of Lappish culture and its origins. In 1752, Leem was appointed Director of a college founded in Trondheim for the instruction of missionaries in the language: the better to cope with this task, he compiled a grammar and a dictionary. He then made translations of the Lutheran Cate-chism and a Book of Common Prayer. All this helped bring the Lapps into the orbit of European civilization, and great credit is due to Leem because his work made things so much easier for the missionaries already in the field, the traders who had already begun to trade with them and the students who were already there observing Lapps on their own ground. Such Lapps as had migrated for good into the mountains remained, of course, beyond the pale; at those altitudes, they were out of reach. They lived on – so we are assured by all the missionaries of the time – in 'outer darkness': led by their shamans, they still made their sacrifices to the mysterious gods of their race.

Fig. 21

Leem's life-work, however, reaped adequate rewards; even if total conversion of the Lapps to Christianity was not achieved, there were many 'settled' Lapps in Norway whom he was able to reach. They could attend at the schools which were now coming into being. He saw the founding of a well-furnished mission-school at Karasjok and a college at Kauto-keino. Leem died in 1774.

On 5 March 1854, the new church at Vittangi, no great distance from the ancient centre of Jukkasjärvi, was taken over by Lars Levi Laestadius, a pastor who certainly left his mark. He fired all the converted Lapps of the Torne region, and the forest-village of Vittangi, with his own fierce brand of puritan-ism, and with the aid of a few disciples he succeeded in

Fig. 21. Shaman of the Nordtröndelag region with a great drum, painted with many designs and figures, and ornamented with stars and circles of copper

reaching a great many families. But the ancient culture suffered at his hands: before very long he and his followers had largely destroyed the Lapps' cultural and artistic heritage.

The paraphernalia of the cult, the magic drums, the daggers, *vetjer*, idols—all were cast into the flames. The old songs were forbidden along with all the old traditional festivals and their games; the feast of *Bâsse-olbmai*, whose origin is lost in the mists of time, and the rest – they were all proscribed as springing from the well of perdition and sin. Men like Laestadius undoubtedly had their merits. The chroniclers hold him to have been a peerless preacher, as puritanical towards himself as he was towards others. But the whole patrimony of an ancient people suffered irreparable damage from such treatment. It says much for the milder and more understanding pastors who succeeded him that the Norwegian Lapps still exist as a people. For so often, when a primitive people such as this is suddenly stripped of its own ancient faith, and its culture is supplanted by the benefits of civilization, disintegration sets in, and the people dwindles and perishes.

PART TWO

THE LIFE OF THE PEOPLE

CHAPTER IV

The Family Group

IN THE WINTRY QUIET of the forests and in their encampments on the outskirts of the villages, the Lapps await the
day of their seasonal assembly, when they can barter their
products for the necessities of life.

In point of fact, great merchandising festivals and fairs are
sometimes held as early as the beginning of February – even in
January in some districts. The men arrive in the villages on
their sleds drawn by fleet reindeer.

These few 'Fair days', provide young people from the
various far-flung clans and families with an opportunity to
come together, which often results in compacts and betrothals.

A Lapp youth whose eye has been caught by a young
woman from a family encamped close at hand will very often
first declare his feelings to her, and then, accompanied by a
friend from her own clan, pay a courtesy call on this neighbouring family. The girl – such is the extreme modesty of the
north – will hurriedly tell her parents about the meeting that has
already taken place at the fair, and the words that were exchanged. Her elders will say nothing. They want to see what
the young man is like before they make up their minds. The
suitor, accompanied by the friend, enters the cabin or the tent
where the girl lives. He pays her some traditional compliment,
then he sits down without ceremony. Rarely is a word ad-
dressed to him. Everyone is looking at the door, apparently
absorbed in what is happening miles away. Should he indeed
be vouchsafed a word or two for his pains, he will take it as a
sign of particular goodwill. He will then ask if he may make
the coffee. Cups and coffee-pot are put before him. Still no
word is spoken. The young woman's parents may refuse to
drink his coffee. That augurs ill for the suitor. All he can do is

get up and bow and make himself scarce for a considerable time. But should the parents, on the other hand, help them-selves to a cup of his coffee with some show of relish, then all is well. The betrothal is to all intents and purposes announced. The friend may congratulate the would-be bridegroom, and the girl can at last stop pretending she is not present.

In some parts of Sweden, in the old days, the suitor used to present himself at the head of a numerous retinue. But only a single member of it, and an elderly one at that, would be at his side when he actually knocked at the door. The pair were awaited by the head of the girl's family, or some other worthy from among her folk. A mutual discussion would then ensue. An argumentive theme ran through it, and it ran to wordiness. Any topic in the world would serve – provided it had nothing to do with the business of the betrothal. Finally the matter would be settled, quite expeditiously, to the accompaniment of demonstrations on the part of the waiting suite. Sometimes these would have been shouting impatiently, to hasten the decision, or even shooting – just a few bullets into the air.

If the suit was accepted, there would be an exchange of gifts and the local alchoholic spirit. The wedding nearly always followed exactly a year later, when the fair came round again.

Then there would be a great gathering in the presence of the village pastor and a great feast, with even strangers welcome. During the ceremonies, one male member of the family would go round with a plate. Each guest would drop money into it and promise to send along, say a reindeer and calf or, according to his means, just the calf: then a youth would take note of all these promised wedding-presents, so that no one should 'forget'. This was more necessary than it sounds. It must be remembered that many marriages were celebrated in the course of these few fair days, so that visitors often found themselves guests at more than one wedding-feast. In fact, they usually made the rounds of all of them, which meant a wedding-present every time. In this fashion, the young couple generally started their life together with a fair-sized herd, not to speak of the reindeer which the bride might have brought as her dowry.

One ancient custom is continued even to this day, nearly everywhere in Lappish territory. The young couple set up house close to the wife's family, in many cases even sharing the parents' tent, although they will naturally prefer to have one of their own. But here we may note again that matriarchal element in Lappish society which we have already encountered in their culture. The tent is in fact the woman's domain – and not in quite the way we might at first think. The implication is rather that it is the mother of the family who is imbued with qualities of steadfastness, of fecundity – in a word, of continuity, the continuity of the stock. It is the mother who must ensure the survival of these Lappish families.

The future bridegroom will have given the girl a ring, which is virtually an engagement ring. On the day of the marriage ceremony, bride and groom exchange rings in the presence of the pastor. The bride now wears two, of exactly similar pattern, adding a third when the first male child is born. Rings are given her on other occasions too: to mark a festival, an anniversary and so on. As a result, many Lapp women have a fine collection. Often, however, they do not wear them, keeping them instead in the *gii'sa*, a little chest that goes into the reindeer's pack-saddle at migration time.

The couple will be faithful to each other. In Lapland, divorce is practically unknown. The great thing in Lappish families is to have children as quickly as possible, so that there will be someone to look after the reindeer when the parents are old. The greatest care is taken of a pregnant woman, and she is treated with every consideration and respect. The husband will study her gait for a hint of whether the coming child will be boy or girl. If the mother-to-be seems to incline a little towards the right, her husband is overjoyed, for it means that a son is on the way. When the great day comes, the husband is banished outside. He may go among his reindeer to hide his fears, talking to them and telling them, as he fondles them, that next winter there will be one little passenger more in the sled.

Nowadays, ceremonies of exorcism have ceased to be performed in the tent, and the shaman is no longer called in to cast good auguries for the birth. The shamans are all dead now, if indeed they are not forgotten. It is a midwife, from the *sii'dâ* itself or from a neighbouring village, who takes the little head in her hands to give it a firm, real Lappish roundness. The infant must on no account have an oblong head like the men from the south.

But until a short while ago, a Lapp woman, particularly if she was a tent-dweller, would see her child into the world without anybody's help, simply kneeling on the ground; at the very most, by way of assistance, she might be supported by one or two other women. This was the custom throughout the Arctic, Eurasia and America alike.

After the advent of missionaries, the babies were baptized. But this did not mean that the Lapps abandoned their older traditions in regard to the naming of the child, though they were careful to see that they did not conflict with the usages of the new religion – except perhaps in one particular. In the privacy of the tent the child would be given the name of a forebear which had been revealed to the mother in a dream. This member of an ancient generation would appear to her and declare his wish for his name to return to the world of the living. If it were given to the new offspring, the ancestor would undertake to bestow his protection on his namesake; he would see that the child grew up strong and came to no harm.

If the mother had had no such dream to inspire her, she might go along to the shaman. The shaman would give a rat-tat-tat on his drum with his little horn hammer, and out would come a name, always a name which had already appeared in the family. If the child had a grandmother living, it would receive from her a little present made of copper. This was an amulet: the boys would wear it in the arm-pit, the girls on their breast. For the mother, this would be a time of celebration. But the father was left out. He was not put out by this, however. He knew well enough that babies and all ceremonies connected with them were a woman's affair.

If in spite of the shaman and his drum and his spells and the grandmother's lucky charms the child still failed to grow up big and strong, the ceremony was repeated – the Lapps saw nothing odd in changing a name. The soul of the ancestor whose name they had first adopted must have failed to find peace: that was their interpretation of events. Perhaps that soul now had its grim dwelling in the heart of some murderous wolf or, for its sins, in a stone. Or it might be prowling about the ice that towered and groaned in distant seas. The child was therefore given a new name, in the hope of a fairer fortune this time.

If all went well and the child grew up hale and hearty, he was given a personal 'mark'. As an adult, he would be entitled to stamp it on his possessions. Children were jealously guarded, and nothing was neglected that might help protect them against the bitter winter cold, and the dangers of a nomad's life following the herds of reindeer.

The Lappish cradle is made from fir or birch. A section of trunk is hollowed out and then covered with skins. There is a covering, like a miniature roof, to protect the baby from the sun, or sudden squalls of rain. The interior resembles a soft fur couch in miniature. The pillow is made from the skin of a reindeer's throat, the softest part. All the other skins used are from young reindeer. Not until the child is some weeks old are these discarded in favour of hare or wolf-pelt.

Plate 15

The weaning stage means separation from the mother for a day or two. When she next gives her child the breast it is

Fig. 22. Three knives of different epochs and from different countries. Left: a flint knife of the Aleutians, sixteenth century; at centre: an Ainu-type knife, also used by the Japanese; on the right, a Lappish bui'ko

blackened with charcoal; the baby turns away and quickly learns to drink from a mug.

The appearance of the first tooth is quite an event. The father, or whoever has made the discovery, gives the child a little reindeer – often the first plaything it ever has. These Lapp children rarely have toys, unless perhaps a doll or two or a miniature sledge carved by their father. The dolls are dressed by the girls of the household: they are put into a replica of Lappish costume which is faithful down to the last ribbon. At two, the boys qualify for a *bui'ko*, a knife of the old Lappish pattern with a lightly curved blade. They start cutting pieces of wood or reindeer-horn. When several children get together their favourite game is mud pies – the building of mud tents and mud cabins to make a real Lappish village. Then they will take it in turns to be king of the castle – or rather chief of an imaginary homestead. But any real desire for such a chieftain-ship will have cooled off in a few years' time.

Lapps are not attracted by the idea of obedience to a chief. Even in the family circle we find shared responsibility and mutual trust between the parents in regard to the children, who represent their faith in the future.

But the young Lapp puts aside childish games at a very early age. In no time at all he is learning to fish, or to go skiing after

Fig. 22

some reindeer that has gone astray. If he does play a game it is a hard and dangerous one – a ski-ride holding on to a reindeer's reins; and the animal chosen is generally a male in its wild state, not a domesticated creature from the herd. This sport has been vividly depicted in many a rock-carving found in North Russia, and on many an ancient drum.

Fig. 4

The girls are very quiet and well-behaved. It is not long before they are out gathering wood, or helping their mother cook or brew coffee. At eight they can tackle any household task like grown-up women.

These Lapp children have quite a happy childhood, or they would were it not for the terrible climatic conditions they have to face over the long winter. The experiment was once made of tempting the Lapps to settle for good and all, in wood cabins heated with fine big stoves. It had a sad outcome: the children were struck down by tuberculosis and died by the score. It was clearly better to let them wander through their woods and mountains with their parents. The various schools for nomads now in existence throughout Lapland wait until they are older before taking them in for the rudimentary in-struction best suited to their needs.

These gentle and obedient pupils are never scolded or struck – or perhaps it is just because they are never punished that they grow up gentle and considerate. Sometimes reaction sets in later, when they start visiting the villages and come into con-tact with people of another race. Then they may well return to their humble camps convinced that they can solve overnight the problems that have baffled their folk for hundreds of years; and start to despise their parents for their failure to better them-selves. This scorn is unjustified, as today there are very few Lapps who do not live in reasonably good conditions, and they have no nagging worries over money.

The fate of the old people, with a relentlessly hard life among the mountains of the north behind them, can be cruel and bitter. The day must inevitably come when they are no longer strong and fit enough to follow the migrations. They are left in the spring encampments, with a few provisions to sustain life, and some fishing gear. Their situation is not an enviable one. An old man or woman, abandoned unarmed in the solitudes of Lapland certainly has small chance of surviving for very long.

A few years ago, homes were started for these old people. But they had little inclination to remain in them. During summer and autumn, they preferred to stay with some family of Lapps settled locally. What their fate was in former times we do not know, but various stories are told which suggest that on occasion the Lapps practised what might euphemistically be termed euthanasia. For instance, an old man, struck down by a sudden fever or incapacitated at last by the intense cold, might find himself plunged into icy water, or hurtling over a precipice in a sled. It is said that the old people themselves sometimes ask for an end to be put to their existence – among the Eskimos as well as the Lapps. But all this is no more than hearsay.

CHAPTER V

Lappish Dwellings

THE LAPPS POSSESS three types of dwelling. Their origin goes back as far as the story of the Arctic peoples itself.

There is the winter dwelling, and there is another for the relatively brief spring and autumn halt which is part of the migration pattern. Finally, there is a third type for the summer, which in all likelihood was always a temporary affair.

This three-fold plan of living is dictated by the habits of the reindeer. Throughout the long winter, the reindeer seeks shelter deep in the forest. With spring, he goes up into the mountains in search of lichens and fungus, coming down again at the onset of autumn. Not all Lapp families are nomads, however, so that we must be careful to make a distinction between the three kinds of dwelling we have mentioned, and the homesteads of the semi-nomads, such as the Skolt tribe, for instance, which until the outbreak of World War II inhabited the Petsamo zone (west of the 'Peninsula of the Fishermen' on the Murmansk coast) and there led a comparatively settled life. As a consequence of frontier changes on the Russo-Finnish border, the Skolts are now dispersed between Lake Inari and the Kola peninsula.

The nomads are almost wholly tent-dwellers. The semi-nomads live mainly in cabins made from branches and from earth, while such clans as have settled down for good in the forests build themselves huts made of tree-trunks, or 'log-cabins'.

The Lapps put up encampments where drinking-water and fire-wood lie to hand. In summer and in between seasons, the nomads' tents are erected on a sunny slope just above the tree-line. We find two varieties of tent. In the more primitive ones a central pole, forked at the end, props up the other poles which

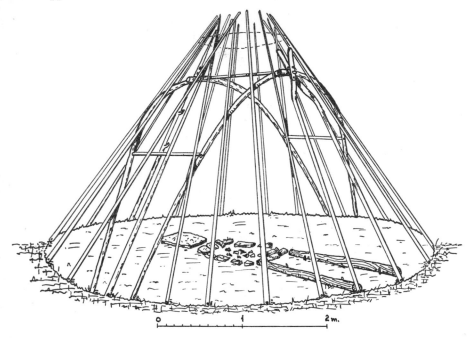

Fig. 23. Framework of a tent of elliptical pattern, with parallel meridian arcs. The fireplace is in the centre

Plate 17

are ranged in a circle. This type is particularly used by the forest Lapps; it is a pattern the Lapps find very practicable when they have to follow in the wake of their herds. Otherwise it is not seen much. It ranks low in Arctic culture and is to be seen among the Samoyeds, the Chukchi and the American Indians. The tents of the 'real nomads' are erected, not on a circular base, but on an elliptical one. Four poles are set in the earth and so placed that they can be curved to form arches, and

Fig. 23

attached in pairs. They then provide support for the other poles. The covering used is the same in each type of tent – large pieces of cloth or reindeer pelts, according to the season.

In the spring and autumn camps, the Lapp homestead

consists of an earthwork cabin and sometimes a *njâllâ* – part of
the real Lappish tradition this, and also to be seen among some
nomads in the Ural zone, such as the Zyryans. The *njâllâ*, as
we have already intimated, is a little wooden cabin usually
mounted upon a pole, or on a tree with its top lopped off, in
which the reindeer meat is stored. Other supplies, like the furs,
stay in the ground-level cabin with its human inhabitants.
The *njâllâ* is reached by a primitive type of step-ladder in the
form of a notched tree-trunk, such as is used by many Arctic
peoples. Sometimes the *njâllâ* is perched upon one of those huge
stones worn smooth by some ancient process of glaciation. The
meat will be as safe on the top of that as on any pole. The
njâllâ was once encountered all over Lapland, but today it is
comparatively rare. The explanation lies in the fact that the
Lapps have begun to put up their spring and autumn camps
near rivers or lakes upon which boats ply, or in the neighbourhood of some halt on the railway that nowadays runs from
Narvik into the very heart of this wild country. With such a
supply line at their disposal, the Lapps' need to store food is no
longer a vital one. In fact at Rensjön, Laimolahti, Vaisaluokta

Plate 21

Fig. 24

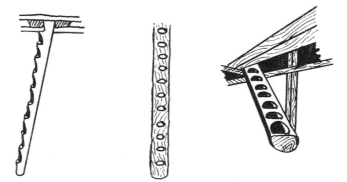

*Fig. 24. Tree-trunks cut for use as steps to serve the sunken dwellings of the Kamchadalo
and Koryaks of North-east Siberia*

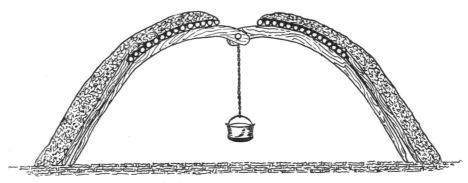

Fig. 25. Section of dome-shaped turf cabin

and Staloluokta in Sweden we find sizable groups of Lapps living for long periods, over the milder months, in cabins that once merely marked the site of the spring camps, and served as nothing more than a temporary halting place for the nomads.

The Ainu, too, as well as the Gilyaks, the Kamchadals, the Yukaghir and the Koryaks used to construct this sort of elevated cabin, rectangular in shape, with a gabled roof to avoid the piling up of the snow, to keep their meat-reserves in. The difference between their *njâllâ* and the Lapp and Zyryan type consisted in the fact that only the latter relied on the single pole as support. And among the Ainu, these elevated cabins grew to a size suggesting human habitation. They stood on a platform supported by quite a number of poles, and sometimes possessed a double-gabled roof. The general aspect suggested some inspiration from the south.

In the Val Camonica, as Marro and Battaglia have pointed out, we also find curious dwellings erected on poles. The characteristic *mazot* of the Vallese is of similar pattern. The kinship between these and the Lapp *njâllâ* suggests that a particular type of construction is adopted where it is necessary to cope with heavy snow.

Lappish tents of both types described above go by the same name, *goatte*. Great care is taken of them. The fire is laid in the centre, in a hearth ringed with stones to keep the glowing embers from spreading. A cauldron hangs over the flames on a chain suspended from a pole which is placed cross-wise, right up in the roof of the tent, where there is an opening for the smoke to escape. If it snows or rains, the Lapps throw a covering over the gap to narrow it.

The tent will usually be about twelve feet across. The hearth is known as the *arrân*; the entrance, a flap between two stakes, goes by the name of *uk'sâ*. The space is divided between the various members of the family, except for one little place behind the hearth and in line with it and the entrance, known as the *boas̆'s̆o*. This is the 'store-cupboard', and it divides the interior into two quite separate compartments. The inhabitants will pass day and night on a fragrant carpet of birch-twigs or fir-branches covered with reindeer pelts. This 'carpet' is renewed once a week; once a day, if there is time, the pelts are given an airing at the opening of the tent. In some parts of Finland a

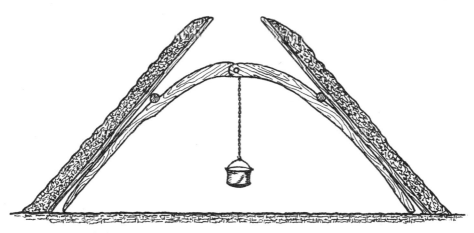

Fig. 26. Section of near-conical type of turf cabin

smaller tent is used. This generally serves just one or two herds-men who have to travel long distances alone in the tracks of the reindeer.

Turf or earth cabins are frequently to be seen in the spring and autumn camps. They are constructed on the same principle as the tents with curved poles forming an arch, but are of course covered with earth and not with canvas or skins. There is the same aperture for the chimney, often fitted with a framework of branches to protect the fire from snow and rain. The door

Plate 20

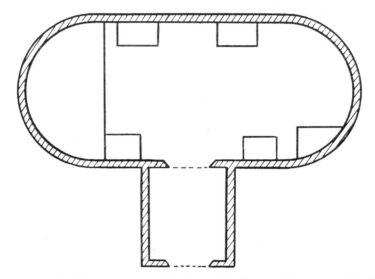

Fig. 27. Plan of a **gamme**—*an archaic form of dwelling, partly below ground-level. This example was discovered at Komagfjord near Hammerfest in Norway. It is reminiscent of many dwellings of northern Siberia and America, and of the Eskimo igloo*

is made of wood, and generally has a chain and padlock. The keys are kept not by the man, but by the woman of the house. She will hang them to a tough-looking leather belt. These cabins, in spring and autumn, provide quarters for the family while the men are out with the reindeer herds. In Swedish Lapland the traveller often comes across them, and they are to be found in Norway too; sometimes they are to be seen in villages of modern construction – old-time survivals now used for storage only. There are two types: domed or conical according to the way the stakes are arranged – as in the case of the tents.

Figs. 25, 26

The forest-Lapps of both Finland and Sweden have from time immemorial built themselves log-cabins or huts. The walls are never very high. In the Vittangi forest, not far from the River Torne, there are some as low as 2 feet 7 inches. Nevertheless, there is plenty of head-room. For not only does the pyramidal or conical roof project upwards from these walls, but very often a sunken floor makes for what is really quite a high-pitched ceiling. The log-cabins are square, and the material used depends on what the region has to offer. Lapps living in the forest belts have built what are virtually small houses, especially in recent times, though they still contain only a single room. They have a boarded floor, but windows are not popular. Windows, and chimneys when they occur are reserved for the dwellings of such Lapps as have altogether abandoned reindeer-herding and the ancient migrations.

There used to be one further type of dwelling, called the *gamme,* quite unlike anything we have described so far. One of these was discovered along the Komagfjord in Norway – a construction, once evidently earth-covered, a good thirty feet long though only five feet high. But the floor was dug well down so that the inhabitants had no difficulty in standing up-right. It was entered by a passage barely three feet high and some ten feet long. In the middle of this cabin were two great stones and the remains of a hearth. Directly overhead was an opening for the smoke. Sleeping-quarters were at the sides, whilst at the back there was a separate sector for a few domestic animals – goats or reindeer, most likely. The door of this *gamme* faced east, thus conforming to a tradition among Arctic peoples that the doors must face either south or east. Semi-

Fig. 27

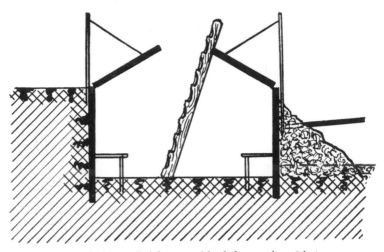

Fig. 28. Section of cabin, partly below ground-level, from northern Siberia

Fig. 28

subterranean cabins on this pattern are still lived in by the Chukchi of North-East Asia, though with them the entrance is sometimes by way of the roof. The Ainu, too, in the Kurile Islands, built such sunken cabins in days gone by. Their entrance, however, was unusual. So far from being a low passage in which one had to stoop, it was more like a spacious entrance-hall. It provided a store-room for arms and for hunting and fishing gear. The dogs slept there at night. A short passage led thence to what was a genuine subterranean dwelling, square in shape, ample in size, and possessing the centrally placed hearth.

Such habitations continued until comparatively recent years in Lapland, and we have a description of one from a Frenchman who certainly did not lack an eye for detail. In his *Relation du Voyage* of 1840, Xavier Marmier writes: 'We made our entry through a door three feet high into a sort of gallery where, from a hole in the roof, a pale ray of light pierced the smoke. To one side a few reindeer pelts composed the entire family couch. On the other side was the stall; in the centre the hearth, and at the back of it a few wooden vessels for the milk. These comprised the only furnishings. A woman with a birch-branch was stirring a cauldron containing fishbones. A girl seated on a stone was making thread, tugging it out of reindeer horn with her teeth and winding it round her knees. Five or six boys, pallid faced, dull-eyed and clearly of poor health, stood in a silent group between this, their elder sister, and their mother.'

Things have greatly changed today. All the settled Lapps, and those who are only half-nomadic, have adopted the log cabin, which does not differ so very much from the farmer's cottage to be seen in southern Scandinavia or the *isba* of the neighbouring Soviet Zone. Moreover, the present-day cabin betrays an artistic sense on the part of its builders. The wood logs, rough-hewn though they may be, are not without carved designs, whilst a distinctive touch is given by a little pediment. They are poles apart from the clumsy shack-type not unknown in the Alps – serving the purpose of a stall or a hay-box and often left untended. In Lapland women tended the cabins, while the man, of course, had the task of choosing the site, which must be conveniently placed for water, and of finding the building material. The fir-trunks used are generally more than roughly of the same diameter; they would stand up to exact measurement.

CHAPTER VI

Hunting and Fishing

EVER SINCE THEY MADE THEIR FIRST APPEARANCE in the human story, the Lapps have shown their mettle at hunting. The first traces we possess of boards attached to the feet for the purpose of traversing wide areas of snow – precursors of the modern skis – relate to the very earliest times: and it is almost certain that they were the invention of the Lapps.

Fig. 10

We have a rock-drawing discovered by Gjessing at Rödöy in northern Norway. It has been dated back to 4,500 years ago, and shows a little man skiing. At Bessov-Noss, too, on the shore of Lake Onega there are carvings which depict men following reindeer on skis. Other skiing figures have come to light at

Fig. 29

Zalavrouga, on the River Vyg, not far from the White Sea and at Bessovi-Scedki. These also are rock-carvings. Actual remains of prehistoric skis have been found all over Scandinavia. Collections can today be seen in various museums – the Nordiska Museum and the Ski Museum at Stockholm, the Västerbotten Museum at Umeå and the Norwegian Ski Museum at Oslo among them.

These prehistoric Lappish skis were rather wider than the modern version and considerably shorter. They were pointed at both ends, and the middle, where there was a raised platform for the foot, was therefore broader. One such primitive 'ski' was found in a tomb in Norwegian Finnmark. The Lappish origin of other objects found in the tomb provided clear proof that the skis too had belonged to some dim ancestor of this race. In one region of North Russia, skis have been discovered of a pattern known as 'Arctic'. These are of relatively recent origin, exactly similar to those in use today among the hunting-peoples of the Urals. A distinction is drawn, however, between these 'Arctic' skis and the 'Bothnian' – that is, the Lappish – type.

Fig. 29. Group of prehistoric skiers from a rock-carving on the Vyg River, near Zalav-rouga, USSR

They belong to different epochs, and are not identical. The zone in which the Lappish type has been found marks the extent of Lappish expansion in Scandinavia: at the same time, the age attributed to these skis tallies with the period when that expansion occurred.

Hunting-prowess on skis can safely be reckoned to have originated in western Eurasia – on all the evidence, about 2000 B.C. There is another opinion, however, which awards the palm to a Mongolian people who were to be found some eight centuries ago between Kirin and Mukden, in what is today Manchuria. This theory was formulated by the Chinese historian Wan-Pun-Son, some years back, in the Thung-Hsi-Pao review. It is a pity that documentary proof is largely lack-ing. There may have been ancient skiers in East Asia but it is only in a few old Japanese pictures that they appear. In these they are bearded figures, drawn along on their skis by reindeer: exactly the same sort of thing can be seen in the rock-carvings near Lake Onega and the White Sea and in northern Norway. What we are evidently dealing with here is the Ainu hunting-people, whose culture belongs to a remote phase of the generalized Arctic culture: and this stemmed without doubt from the sub-glacial regions of the north, as we shall see.

My own humble opinion is that the racket-shoe, rather than the ski, properly belongs to the Asiatics. It was unknown to the Lapps and the Samoyeds, yet in use from the remotest times in North-Eastern Asia, as among the American Indians and the Eskimos. It may well be that the Asiatics found the racket-shoe better suited to their needs than the ski, though the ski too came into use later on. The Asiatics were hunters only and they relied on the ambush-technique. The Lapps, at the other extremity of the great land-mass, from being mere hunters became herdsmen, following where the reindeer led. For such protracted movement, the ski was ideal.

Fig. 30. Painting on the skin of a drum, showing a Lappish skier armed with a bow

In all fairness, however, we should draw attention to the extraordinary resemblance between some Gilyak skis and the Lapp pattern. Von Schrenk was the first to remark on this. Nor should we fail to point out that some hunters and fisher-folk at the mouth of the Amur, in northern Sakhalin, have skis which are wide and short and raised to take the foot in the middle – this in a region where the other tribes use the racket-shoe also. But, then, this might be due to the influence of the neighbouring Ainu people.

As early as A.D. 780 we find Paulus Diaconus[1] recording that the Lapps slide along on two bow-like pieces of wood, hunting wild animals. And in 1555 the Swedish priest Olaus Magnus in his *Historia de Gentibus Septentrionalibus* wrote:[2] 'They tie their slides to their feet and hold in the hand a stick wherewith to guide themselves. Combining running and jumping, they can descend the snowy mountain slope follow-ing the wild beasts.' Johannes Schefferus, too, in 1673 speaks of the Lapps as hunters swiftly following the reindeer on skis.[3]

A rather simple hunting-procedure was thus described by Francesco Negri: 'They pull after them a lump of ice or wood, whose motion along the ice makes much noise. Hearing this

beside him, the beast will be fearful and turn his head to find
out what can be the cause of such din. But in doing so, he will
forget to raise his legs to a sufficient height and stamp with
sufficient force to sustain his motion over the ice. In consequence, he will slip and fall. Whereat the hunter has his
chance to attack. The fallen beast will try to rise, but cannot.
Or if he does, he may not swiftly get back into his stride. He is
the hunter's prey.'[4]

We have already seen how the reindeer drew a whole
people in the wake of their trek from the southerly regions they
had certainly occupied for centuries to the very northernmost
limits of Europe. In great, close herds they explored valley after
valley for lichen-grazing. The Lapps therefore, took up their
stand at clearings, in narrow strips of woodland, at fords or
river beds, and there set their *vuobmân* – a form of palisading or
fencing, an avenue of stakes and branches sometimes extending
over miles. Towards the end it narrowed, and reindeer which
had run into the trap found themselves herded into an enclosure, or *gar'de,* where they were finally caught. The difficulty
of the procedure lay in inducing the herd to enter the mouth of
the *vuobmân*. This meant relentless beating and driving, and
man had to move faster on the snow than the reindeer.

*Fig. 31. Painted on the skin
of a drum, this schematized
or stylized design represents
a vuobmân—the enclosure
into which the Lapps drove
the wild reindeer*

A tamed reindeer, specially trained for the purpose, played
its part in the early stages. Its role was to act as decoy, so to
speak, for the wild animals. On a very long leash it was posted
at the mouth of the *vuobmân:* and slowly, led by the good
grazing, it would munch its way in the desired direction.
Others would follow – into that wide avenue of stakes and
branches which led into the trap. This 'decoy' process became
a much easier matter if the time of year permitted the Lappish
hunters to have at their disposal a stallion, or a female in season.
In some zones, if the enticing was done by a male, strapping
would be applied to its antlers. This was a cunning device
which ensured that if a wild male from the approaching herd,

G

attacked, the two duellers would be unable to draw apart. The tame animal would then try to manœuvre the other into the *vuobmân*. The whole herd would naturally follow two males in combat. At the decisive moment, the hunters would step in, driving this splendid catch deeper into the trap. And instead of lurking in ambush to destroy the herd – as the Eskimos and the Indian caribou-hunters do to this day – they would trap the reindeer alive, and so pen him up.

Fig. 32. Two stylized drum-figures of Lapp archers

The Lapps had also learned to set traps for lone animals. The trap generally took the form of a trip-wire to catch the feet or the antlers, and was slung between two stunted northern trees.

Various weapons were used for hunting. Chief among these was the bow – a primitive bow of which one single example has come down to us. It is preserved in Orbyhus Castle in Sweden. It is of a type described by Schefferus as belonging to the sixteenth century – and later the description is amplified by Linnæus, and other students of the Lapps. They called it 'the Asiatic type' – not the most faithful description, perhaps, even when amended by Manker to read 'North Asiatic'.[5] A better classification has come from the Finnish ethnographer T. I. Itkonen: in a conversation with Manker he proposed 'Finno-Ugrian'.

The very simplicity of this bow sets it apart from others. It consists of two parts. The outer arc is birchwood, and there is an inner and shorter one of pine, to give the bow increased strength and elasticity. The Orbyhus bow measures 5 feet $9\frac{5}{8}$ inches and is at no point more than 1 inch thick. The missing cord (it would almost certainly have been animal sinew) was fitted into notches at each end. The bow was once tightly sheathed in coils of fibre obtained from birchbark, wound round its entire length. One end of the bow is iron-tipped. Possibly it had a secondary use as a weapon for defence at close quarters, or else it may have also served as a ski-stick. The earliest arrows used with a bow of this type were bone-tipped. Later on, the Bronze Age and the Iron Age saw a certain evolution in arrows as in other things. With the development of metallurgy – which did not reach Lapland until comparatively late in the day – an important part was played by a sword-tip for use against the wolf and a long, lance-like shaft for the bear. The sword-tip was itself tipped with iron – one more hint of a double use as a ski-stick, for the arrow this time. The point of the lance-tip was protected by a little cap made from reindeer horn.

The Lapps did not confine their hunting to reindeer. They were nimble hunters of bear too and, above all, of elk. Smoked and kept in special conditions, in a little store-room of seasoned wood, elk is very tasty.

Cormorants were hunted ceaselessly. The Lapps would snare them as they floated on the calm waters of the lake. With great ingenuity, the birds were 'trailed for' with something like a spinner – a piece of wood or leather shaped like a fish and bristling with hooks. The birds would naturally follow and fall on the lure with open beak. Once hooked, they were drawn into the bank with the aid of a long flexible stick. The Eskimos of Hudson Bay still use very similar methods.

In the vast forests, the Lapps still snare ptarmigan and, up in

Fig. 33. Wild-fowling as represented in a drum-picture

Fig. 33

the mountainous regions, Arctic partridge. In marshy districts, wild duck used to be considered the pick of the bag. The Lapps went after it with a kind of boomerang called the *ballak* – which bears a remarkable resemblance to the bone *vogelpfeils* discovered during excavations in the great peat-bog of Magle-möse, in the Danish island of Sjælland. This dig yielded many similar throwing weapons – in addition to light arrows of the type used for birds, clubs, axes and maces, all of early Neolithic date.

Not till later, when their commercial value came to be appreciated, did the hunt turn on hare, fox and lynx. The wolverine probably began to be hunted a little earlier – as soon as the Lapps had reindeer to protect, for the 'glutton' was an enemy of the herds, and fond of making night attacks. For him the following simple trap was devised: from a cord slung between stakes was suspended a sharp knife, and below it a piece of meat. Once the 'glutton' had started sniffing round the meat, sooner or later he was bound to brush against the stakes, and down would drop the blade on his head.

When the Lapps learned of the cross-bow, they turned their attention to a good many more birds, and hunted down badger, otter and ermine.

The actual bow of the Lappish cross-bow was worked in iron. In some districts the very same thing can still be seen – but only in the form of a small-scale model, made as a toy bow for the children.

Here is a seventeenth-century description of the cross-bow as used by the Lapps:[6] 'The instrument favoured for such hunting by this people and its neighbours is the big cross-bow having an arc of iron. It may not be wound by hand. The method is to turn it over, and holding it down on the ground, charge it with one foot. The hunters release the cord by means of an iron hook, which they carry for this purpose, attached to their belts. The bow fires no sharp dart or ball, but a shaft of wood as thick as a finger, yet of three times that thickness at the end, which is turned to bell or pyramid shape for the tip.'

The cross-bow was no stranger to other Arctic races within the orbit of the higher cultures of the south. It was often adapted to quite complex uses, as the following example will show. A trap for the bigger animals – bear, elk, reindeer, wolf – was contrived from a stake planted in the earth with a cord attached to it. This cord was connected to the 'trigger' of a cross-bow concealed a few paces away, the arrow it held being pointed at the stake. A passing animal touched the cord. This released the little wooden trigger, causing the arrow to be fired. Traps of this type were to be seen in Lapland and in the Russian Ural Mountain zone. The Rev. J. Batchelor found similar ones among the Ainu.

All Lappish families have a dog, and he shows his mettle no less in guarding the herd than in hunting. The animal is of middling size with large, pointed ears and a keen, intelligent expression – the picture of devotion and trust. Should a rein-deer escape and start making off to the mountains again, one glimpse is enough for the dog: it will be brought back. One Lappish legend has it that man and the dog have from the earliest times entered into a mutual pact. The dog helps man with his hunting and his reindeer-tending: man gives him his daily bread. When finally the dog is too old and feeble to track a wolf or bear across the snow, or to follow the uncertain spoor of a runaway reindeer through a marsh, then man must put an end to his friend's life by hanging him from a tree. This the Lapps used to do, but with tears in their eyes, and not until the old dog's place had been taken by a younger one.

On the Lapps' methods of fishing, Negri has written: 'The Lapps use both net and hook for their fishing. They barter their own products for these implements, but can on occasion show skill in making them with their own hand: the nets being woven of stripped osier, the hooks a twig of a simple L-shape,

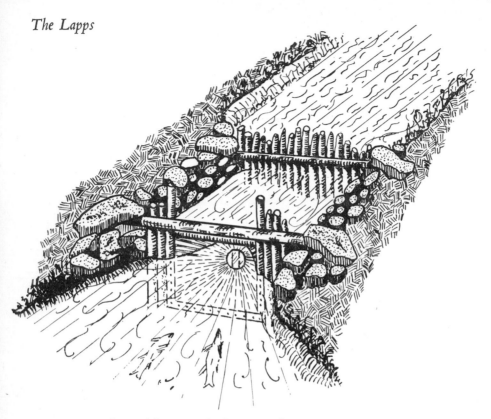

Fig. 34. A typical Lappish barrier-trap for the narrows of rivers

sharpened at all its points.'

Today, few means other than the net are used to take the trout, salmon and sea-trout which are to be found in such abundance in the rivers and lakes of Lapland. A boat with an outboard motor is a very common sight up in the mountain lakes. It will shoot out into deep water at speed, and then the fisherman will stop and cast. Behind this gesture lies a long tradition, and it is tradition, too, which dictates his dress – the blue cloak of the multi-coloured appliqué strips. But nowadays, the cloak is almost as messy with oil and petrol as any mechanic's. There are few regions left where the real old-time methods are still followed. These are certainly more interesting to watch than a rapid operation with a motor-boat. A line that bristles with a whole host of little bone needles is used. The needles are covered with bait, and the line is laid along the bottom. When the fish takes it, the sharp pieces of bone catch in its mouth. It is an age-old method, but it is still practised throughout Arctic Eurasia and the far north of America. There is also the barrier-method, in which a barricade is placed across the narrows of a river known to be rich in salmon. Into it had been worked a mass of such little spears of bone, and these were similarly loaded with bait.

These ancient fishing-methods have by no means died out in northern Norway along the Arctic Coast, where a short time ago bone hooks and barricades of all types, some of them highly ingenious, were still being widely used. But in Sweden, Lappish fisher-folk are becoming progressively fewer. Fishing has turned into a mere sport for a few forest-Lapps –a pleasurable change from reindeer-tending, and little more. Not that tending the herds means such hard work for them, there being no migrations on any scale. For the mountain-Lapps too, fishing has tended to become no more than a pastime. Old men are devoted to it: so are children. But the average adult is not enthusiastic. In this modern age he feels that there is something singularly unflattering about the epithet 'fisher-folk'.

Fig. 34

Chapter VII

Reindeer-Breeding

LAPP ECONOMY REMAINS almost wholly based on the reindeer. In spite of a present-day tendency to devote less time, and less surface area, to reindeer-breeding, it can still be said to absorb a greater share of the Laplander's life than anything else.

These powerful antlered animals have a pelt of brown or reddish-brown which thins out a little in winter. Shoulder height is about three feet. They vary in weight. Some males approach the two cwt. mark, but for the most part they are lighter – and exceedingly nimble. The antlers branch out in a fashion which is asymmetrical rather than absolutely regular. Both sexes are horned, but the male the more heavily of the two. In no other animal of this type is the female horned. But this is not the only difference between the reindeer and its cousins. A reindeer's antlers start to grow when it is thirty days old; in any other type of deer such growth is delayed nine or twelve months. The reindeer's antlers, and their early growth, set the species apart. The female keeps her antlers up to the month of May, when she gives birth to her young, and she goes without them till September. The male loses his when a thick carpet of winter snow lies over the tundra – about the end of November. The reindeer's antlers are not so large as those of kindred species, but they can still be magnificent. A pair will sometimes number twenty-five points.

In the latitude where reindeer live, winter can last eight or nine months. It is a hard time for the animals. They are forced to go down into the forests, whose floors are naturally less densely covered with snow, with so many branches to break its fall. Lichen is easier to find there. Even so, a particularly heavy fall can bury it too deep. Then, desperate for food, the reindeer leaves the forest and makes for the wind-beaten hills.

His vain search for lichen-pasture will often drive him to the very edge of the land.

When the fairer weather returns and the ice thaws, the reindeer become restive and one fine day they will start for the heights, ploughing through the mud, picking their way slowly but surely over melting ice – and followed at every step by man. From the river valleys they will climb to their green browsing on the mountain-side, far from the midges and mosquitoes which are the scourge of the brief tundra summer. Up there, fresh breezes and frequent rain keep the lichen fresh, and the Lapp, after his own hard winter in the forest, plants his tent near the best pastures, where the reindeer likes to pause. But all of a sudden, without warning, the herd will be off in search of fresh pastures. Though the reindeer's itinerary over the mountains may seem very haphazard, these animals are actually following trails almost certainly blazed in ancient times. Very rarely do they deviate from these, their appointed paths of migration. The region crossed by the great herds in spring and autumn is one for which the Lapps have an apt name. They call it the 'Blessed Land of Rana-Nei'dâ', after the goddess of flowering plants and the good season. Here, too, dwelt ancient primitive man whom the nomads have personified as *Varalden-Olbmai*, 'Earth-man', who still endows the reindeer with fecundity: because it is in this land, his ancient domain, that they give birth to their young.

The reindeer, in their migration, exchange their pine forest for a forest of dwarf birches, scattered thinly in a belt that lies from 2,000 to 3,000 feet above sea-level in Swedish territory, but distinctly lower in Norway and Finland. They will roam it without a pause till they come to their grazing, climbing to the crests of mountain slopes still snow-covered even during the warmer hours of the day. Of course there are many Lappish reindeer-breeders whom the migration-season never takes to these mighty mountains. The herds belonging to some of the

Norwegian groups make for the Atlantic coast in spring, while those of the more northerly groups in Finland move towards the Petsamo coast.

At the first sign of returning cold, the herds come down once more, still by way of the ancient trails. For a short while they will break the journey at the place where they paused in the spring⁄time to have their young. Then they move off once more – back into the forest and its wintry silence. The cycle is complete.

We have seen how the Lapps, though for long they were only a hunting⁄people, are yet very old hands at domesticating the reindeer. In actual fact they may since earliest times have kept a few head, even when the herd at large ran wild. We have gathered something of their methods of capturing the animal – by using a 'decoy' reindeer and the *vuobmân,* with its enclosed pen and one⁄way passages, and other traps.

Even today, the reindeer have scarcely reached their new mountain⁄pastures or their 'land by the sea' before the herds⁄men are rounding them up using the time⁄honoured method and sorting out of the throng animals which may belong to a different owner. The 'brand⁄mark' is nicked into the animal's ear with a hunting⁄knife soon after its birth. Such marks are recognized, and legally registered today, but in the past the only purpose they served was to put an end to squabbling between claimants. Hugo A. Bernatzik,[7] on his return from a journey through the Västenjaure zone in 1934, recorded the existence of eighteen different basic marks and an unlimited scope for combinations!

These marking operations used generally to be undertaken in the milking⁄season – an annual event only with reindeer – and a few forest⁄Lapps in the Vittangi district still perform them at this time. They construct a circular pen and all round it light fires of peat which they keep going with the aid of

Plate 23

resinous pine cut down into kindling-wood. Only in such conditions, the Lapps maintain, will reindeer allow you to milk them. Young boys have the duty of keeping the fires burning, and the ring of fire must be maintained at all costs. More fuel is put on all the time to give backing and make a fine pall of smoke. The stage is now set for the ear-marking of the young reindeer, which takes place while the women go off to make the cheese. The men will have seen to it that the animals have gone a whole day without food; any would-be browser feels a touch of the whip. Not until the next morning, at the time-honoured hour of ten o'clock, are they allowed out of the pen to graze.

The female reindeer does not make a good mother. Often enough, the young calves find themselves completely aban-doned, and left by the herd they are attacked by wolves. But in regions where the reindeer is the captive of man, dogs and herdsmen keep a good watch and see that the animals stay together. In Sweden, up in the high grazing-lands, one can see hundreds of reindeer humbly following in the footsteps of a big castrated male with a bell tied to him.

Just before she gives birth, the reindeer seeks out some isola-ted spot – for preference, a rugged mountain crag where she can go through her labour-pains without being the object of curious glances. At such a time the whole herd will always be inclined to restlessness, knowing only too well the danger from prowling wolves. It is not always the wolf, however, that lies in wait. There is another redoubtable enemy – the eagle. When a solitary reindeer is looking for a place to drop her calf, her comings and goings are watched from the sky. Time and time again, the great bird of prey will come down and take up his perch on a steep bank, ready to swoop. Many reindeer flee the spot the moment their labour is over, and an effortless slaughter follows. These faint-hearted reindeer-mothers the Lapps call *suop'pa*. If the calf can be recovered alive it is hanged.

But the herd does not lack for defenders either, some of them from its own ranks. For not only men and dogs but the rein-deer themselves watch over its destiny: old males, their muzzles worn smooth with all the browsing they have done in ice and snow, their half-blind eyes big and heavy with a tired, rheumy look, seem to develop a sixth sense which enables them to scent all and every danger.

An old male reindeer is, however, liable suddenly to go crazy. He will then let out a terrible bellow, and go plunging round and round till he collapses. The others flee in terror; whereupon their deserted companion is killed if he is in cap-tivity, or left to the wolves if he is wild. There are Lapps who claim this *oai've-vikke,* as they call these attacks, can be cured by cutting off the tip of the afflicted animal's tail. Reindeer are liable to numerous other scourges too, some of which are cured in a most unorthodox manner. A reindeer suffering from inflammation of the urethra, for instance, is made to drink human urine which has been collected in a vessel containing a piece of sealskin with every trace of hair removed.

Lapps will slaughter their reindeer only when their smoked meat reserve, or their food supplies in general, are in danger of running-out. Their first choice will be a sick animal; alterna-tively, they will slaughter a sterile doe, or an enfeebled male. Autumn, before the rutting season, is the best killing time. The meat is tenderer and tastier then, at this season of the *sârves.* The lean flesh is dried, and hung in the tent, where wreaths of smoke from the hearth will play round it – a simple but effective way of smoke-curing. Until only a short time ago, the meat was then put away in a *njâllâ* – the 'ice-box' perched up on a pole or a rock—where it remained until the following spring, when the caravan of men and reindeer would again be in the neighbourhood; for where the caravan had rested in autumn, it invariably returned for the spring sojourn – after that inexorable migration from winter-camp to winter-camp.

In former times, the nomads made an attempt to advance the milking-season to the last few days of June – they would have liked to see it coincide with the Feast of St John (Midsummer), a favourite time of celebration once they had been converted to Christianity. This, however, proved to be a bad mistake. Reindeer milked at this time, and for several days running at that, gave very little yield, sometimes merely a few drops. And all the while the calves had to be kept off or muzzled with a kind of nose-bag.

Manker has made a long study of the techniques and the periodicity of reindeer-milking among the Swedish mountain-Lapps.[8] He believes that the terms the Lapps use in connection with milking show a definite affinity to their Nordic equiva-lents. This confirms an opinion generally held that the Lapps learned to milk reindeer only after they had seen cows being milked by their neighbours to the south.

As against that, it should be remembered that all Lapps, Norwegian, Swedish, Finnish and Russian, have their own independent Lappish word for 'the milking', while the word they use for the milk itself is *miel'ke* – clearly of Germanic origin. It seems unlikely, to say the least, that a people like the Lapps, reindeer-breeders from early times, did not hit on the idea of milking their herds until it was suggested to them by the men of the south.

When it is simply a question of quenching a thirst, the Lapps to this day, like any other Arctic people, drink the milk straight from the reindeer's udders. The Samoyeds are said to go further, and cut a vein to suck the blood. Of recent years, however, in the interests of the young reindeer, the Lapps have taken to keeping goats near their camping grounds, both for their milk and the cheese they make from it.

Reindeer-breeding is no easy occupation, and involves far more than the effort of following a herd to its grazing-grounds. The herdsmen must be on the alert all the time, they must know what to do and seize the exact moment in which to do it, if the herd is to be kept in tip-top condition. And this is necessary if it is to 'pay its way'. The reindeer is very particular about its feeding – it has very definite tastes. It demands its own chosen lichen and is perfectly able to tell it apart from all others; except in winter, with all the pasturage under snow, when it will be thankful to browse at the first patch it can turn up as it scratches away with its hoof. For the most part it will insist on a variety known as *Cladonia rangiferina*. In summer, however, the *Cladonia* which grows on the plains dries up with the heat of the sun. The animals cannot eat it, and so they migrate in spring. They are in search of regions where squalls of rain keep the earth soft and the lichen fresh. While they are crossing a zone of poor grazing, reindeer will nibble at buds, birch-leaves, sorb-apple leaves, willow, and so on. At times reindeer feed on fungus; in a humid region, they resort to it frequently.

And behind the reindeer, plodding along at his heels, man keeps going – over mountain and valley, tackling stretches of ice, fording swirling rivers. And when spring comes round and the does give birth, his efforts are rewarded. This marks the beginning of the cycle. For the Lapps it may not mean riches, but it means survival.

The mating-season, which the Lapps call *râgâd-ai'ge*, lasts about six weeks, beginning usually between 20th and 30th September each year – that is, immediately after the necessary slaughtering – and its end marks the onset of the long winter. The males become highly excitable and the herdsmen have their hands full coping with animals who wander in the course of their mating or during fights. The male can at this time turn very fierce – sometimes to the extent of killing the doe. The herdsmen, too, have to watch out that they do not get hurt. If he is not careful, a man will find himself gored in the shoulder –

and then, before he can escape, his kidneys will be hammered by the animal's hind legs. That is when he needs his dog by him. The dog seems to be able to sense the reindeer's mood, and anticipate any aggressive move by itself attacking first. Without a dog close by, the only thing the herdsmen can do is clamber up a tree or on to a rock. Many stories are told about herdsmen having to stay in such a refuge for hours, or even days, at a time – until his companions have got a rope round the attacker. When captured, it is at once castrated and deprived of its antlers, which are broken off. Castration is effected with the teeth. For some unknown reason, the Lapps are loth to use a knife and certainly the animal appears to make a more rapid recovery if the genitals are bitten off. The same method of castration is used by the Samoyeds. The traveller De Lesseps, writing in 1790, recorded a similar practice among the Kamchadals, for dogs.

There has always been a good deal of speculation about reindeer-breeding, and this is what Renato Biasutti[9] has to say on the subject:

'The northern habitable zone of Eurasia has a history all its own; this is the region which took in the reindeer- and mammoth-hunters when they were following up the receding ice and the sub-polar fauna. These men brought with them the early artifacts of their primitive culture (it was the era of the boomerang and the crudest prototype of the bow and arrow) into the far north. The zone was then further enriched by a wave which reached it from the more advanced southerly regions. There thus came into being a Neolithic culture of hunters and fisher-folk. Agriculture was not practised. Archaeologists have brought many traces of this age to light. Their discoveries form part of the heritage of Eurasian Arctic and sub-Arctic culture. Furs for human wear, sled-dogs, sleds, racket-shoes, fish-spears and tent-cabins of conical form offer the main evidence of an era of Shamanism, the Bear-Cult, the burial on raised ground, sexual hospitality to guests and group-marriage. One of the later achievements of this epoch was stock-breeding, on whose origins the theories of E. Hahn can still be regarded as very sound. Stock-breeding, Hahn maintains, derived from the agrarian culture of southern Asia, working its way northward. The first species to be domesticated were those indigenous to the temperate and the sub-tropical steppe. The last species was the reindeer. In all likelihood, as Montandon suggests, the Lapps were the first to tame the reindeer. The new practice then spread eastward, but the handling of the animals grew less and less skilful the farther east it went. Tarando-pastoral culture, as it has been called, is a mixed product whose components are both Arctic and pastoral. A contrary opinion is held by Schmidt and Koppers. They hold that nomadic stock-breeding began with the reindeer, and then worked its way south, being applied to different animals as it went. No possible foundation exists for this belief. Archaeological investigations near Lake Ladoga prove to us that as late as the Neolithic Age – and when it was well under way – the inhabitants of the region were hunters pure and simple. They possessed dogs of two kinds, but the dog was their only domesticated animal. In these parts, reindeer ran wild and they were hunted. That is still true to this day of the Kamchadals, the Eskimos and the Athabaskan Indians.'

Manker, however, felt it necessary to draw attention to one important feature of W. J. Raudonikas's imposing collection of rock-drawings. All these came to light in the region between Lake Onega and the White Sea.[10] Some of the figures portrayed are more easily accounted for if we accept the theory of reindeer-breeding existing at least in some rudimentary form, as it is difficult to explain them as mere hunting-scenes. Some of the graffiti for instance show a man on skis attached to a reindeer. They bear a striking resemblance to the little

Fig. 35. Lappish type of pack-saddle, consisting of two curved boards fitted together at the top

pictures on Lappish drums. Manker is careful not to deny that the man on skis may only be hunting reindeer. But he is anxious that students should not miss the possible implications of this prehistoric evidence.

He is equally anxious that the student should neglect no aspect of such finds as are unearthed. In the case of utensils, it is important to know for instance whether they are made from bone or horn, and just where they were discovered. One such discovery gave us striking evidence of the antiquity of reindeer-breeding – namely the spade-ended ski-sticks. Scholars are all agreed on the reason for the sticks being of that particular pattern: their purpose was to enable the herdsman to dig about in the snow, helping the reindeer in his eager search for pasturage. A ski-stick and a pair of skis found in 1924 near the village of Kalvträsk (in Sweden) have thus established a date, by pollen-analysis, which is startlingly early: 2000 B.C. Ostyaks and Zyryans of today use a similar spade-ended stick. Reindeer-breeding may indeed be so ancient as to have begun even before the first appearance of the Lapps in Scandinavia.

Figs. 5, 6

The archaeologist's most significant finds, however, in this regard, need not be in the nature of implements, utensils, weapons and so on. Bone and horn can provide valuable, and sometimes exact information. Bones broken by thrown weapons – such as arrows or lances – can be distinguished

H

from bones broken with, say, a club or a slaughtering knife: though in the latter case we are unfortunately unable to tell whether or not the animal was already held in a trap or pen prepared for the purpose of slaughter.

But the antlers tell a story which leaves us far less in doubt. *Figs. 35, 36* Castration, which enabled man to use the male reindeer (by far the more robust) as pack-beast and sled-animal, left clear traces in the form of an anatomical modification in the antler-bases. This discovery of a male cranium showing a convex surface-form at the antler base or one horn with concave

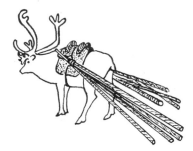

Fig. 36. Reindeer carrying tent-poles in the course of a migra-tion

grooving shows that castration had by then been introduced and that therefore, the male reindeer could by then have been put to domestic uses. Moreover, as Manker has pointed out, the very fact that castration is performed by the teeth is proof that the practice started in a rude and ancient age.

To sum up, we may say that all the evidence points to the Lapps themselves having originated the reindeer-breeding they have always lived by. The entire tradition of it, in every aspect, gives no hint of outside influence. Most important of all, the reindeer's double role – draught animal in winter, beast of burden in summer – is typical of this culture alone, as is the milking.

With regard to the dogs, it must be emphasized that they have one job to do and one only: to look after the herds. All over the Arctic they are put to the sled – but not in Lapland. Nor have they been used for the *travois* – a system of transporting goods which consists in trailing poles from the animal's sides, or from a special saddle, and then securing the bundles on the poles.

One more characteristic feature of reindeer-breeding which is exclusively Lappish is to be seen when the animal is slaughtered. Among the Norwegian, Finnish and Russian groups, the blow is struck into the heart with a slaughtering-knife; in Sweden, it is plunged into the back of the neck. We know that the Samoyed and other races in the Soviet Union kill their reindeer by strangulation.

Here, in the use of the knife, is an aspect of reindeer-culture which is exclusively limited to the Lapps. When we consider it in conjunction with all the long and meticulous care that goes into the domestication of the animal; when we contrast the success achieved by the Lapps with the very indifferent results obtained by Siberian and Uralic races – whose herds still run half-wild or quite untamed, – then we can appreciate the innumerable generations of skill which must lie behind the reindeer-culture of Scandinavia, and must come to the conclusion that the Lapps alone could have been its initiators.

CHAPTER VIII

Clothes, Handiwork, Food and Drink

O N THE STAGE OF RECORDED HISTORY, the Lapps first appear draped in animal skins. Their main activity was reindeer-hunting. There can be little doubt that the reindeer pelts furnished the first rudimentary clothing they wore.

Up to quite recent times, Lapps of the central and southern zones kept the reindeer-skin blouse known as the *svaltja* for summer wear. In the north they merely used an old skin with a hole in the middle for the head and a belt to keep it in at the sides. The result was not unlike the South American *poncho*.

Modern dress comprises headgear of a type which varies with the locality, a blouse of almost uniform pattern through-out Lapland, and trousers narrowing at the calf. Most authori-ties agree that it is medieval in inspiration, with a definite Viking influence in the decorative touches.

Fig. 37

The blouse is generally known as the *gak'te* (*kolte* in some northern districts). It is really a kind of coat reaching half-way down the thigh (as worn by women it comes down below the knee). With it goes a leather belt studded with big metal discs. It is nearly always blue, though red and white can also be seen sometimes in Norwegian Finmark. In ancient times, white was decreed for the womenfolk on festival days and holi-days. In the north, the blouse opens a little at the neck only. Elsewhere, among the Swedish forest-dwelling Lapps and those of the Jokkmokk zone, it can be opened all the way down for the men, but not for the women. The men may also wear it with a semi-stiff collar. This has now disappeared from the female costume, though women wore it too at one time.

But the really attractive and interesting part of Lappish dress is the multicoloured ribboning or braid-work – the prevalent colours are yellow and red – which is worn round the neck

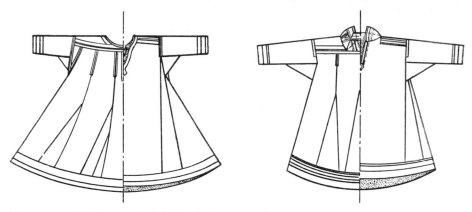

Fig. 37. Lappish blouses; on the left, the collarless type; right, a type at one time repre-senting a widespread fashion but now less popular

and wrists, and on the shoulders. It also forms the hem of a blouse.

It would be of great interest to know whether these decora-tive touches really spring from medieval dress or whether they reached the Lapps from such Arctic-littoral races as the Samoyeds, the Yakuts, the Tungus, the Chukchi, the Ainu, the Eskimos and the rest. The fact that they are more frequently to be seen in the northern districts does perhaps suggest the latter. A close study of dress among these peoples will show them to be equally fond of bright colours, worn to make a man visible at distance against snow. The Mongolians also knew the practical value of high colour. Their *kulat* was blue, and bore a striking resemblance to the Lapp *gak'te*. Colour was also used with the same purpose in mind among some Tibetan peoples.

The Ainu costume, which is very similar to that of the Lapps, has its ornamental touches, especially at the neck, on the back, and at the hem of the sleeves and the skirt. The decorative theme used is often a stylized bear's head. The entire costume will sometimes be covered with them. George Montandon[11] brought one back from the Piratori, in which

Fig. 38

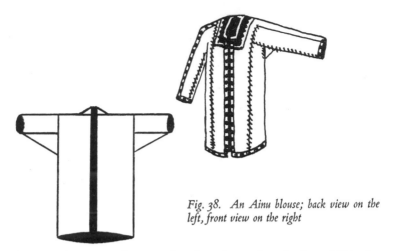

Fig. 38. An Ainu blouse; back view on the left, front view on the right

the motifs repeat those to be found on the cloaks of North-West American Indians. From the Kurile Islands, too, this author brought a costume in every way similar, even down to the colouring, to the type worn by the Lapps.

Beneath the *gak'te*, at one time the Lapps wore a garment called a *lii'vâ*: later its place was taken by the modern vest or flannel shirt. But the *lii'vâ*, sometimes worked with a kind of shiny tinsel, is still worn in some southern zones on great occasions.

The trousers – *buk'sâ* – are narrow and can be closed up again under the feet. They, too, can be made of reindeer skin. Formerly they were worn by Lapp women as well as men: but today, in the south especially, they prefer to model themselves on their Scandinavian sisters and wear a long blue gown. Lappish trousers were adopted by Nordic peoples when they took to the ski, being very suitable for wear in snow. The Lapps used skin or cloth 'puttees' to bind them close to the calf, in order to keep the snow out of their shoes.

Fig. 39   The latter were a kind of heel-less moccasin called *gâbmâgâk*. They were made from three pieces of reindeer-skin sewn together with cord obtained from reindeer sinews. The lower part and the upper part met in a curved point at the front – in a fashion reminiscent of oriental slippers and certain medieval types of shoe. It is possible, however, that this curved point served a very definite purpose – to facilitate the attachment of skis. Manker and Elgström are among the authorities who hold this view. For their winter footwear, the Lapps prefer to use skins taken from the reindeer's legs: the sole, however, may consist of skin off the cranium. This is readily distinguished by the thickness of the hair, and is extremely durable. The Lapps have discovered, too, a means for rendering this sole absolutely waterproof. The mountain nomads cut a round hole in it which they fill with a ring of hard leather. This cannot stretch, and when weight is put on it during the action of walking the skin around it is tensed. As a result the sole is stretched taut and becomes waterproof.

Fig. 39. Two styles of moccasin: on the left, the type worn all the year round by the Lapps; on the right, the type worn by the Chukchi and Palæo-Siberians generally

The Lapps wear no stockings or inner covering for the foot. Instead, they simply take some dried grass – *suoi'dne* – and put sufficient of it into the shoe to cover the whole foot. This grass, *Carex vesicaria,* is found growing under willows or in marshy ground. It is put under pressure, or combed out or beaten on stone to keep it from becoming limp. Then it is plaited and put into storage. It has one great advantage: it can be dried before the fire in the space of a few seconds. It was used with excellent results in F. Nansen's polar expedition of 1893–6.

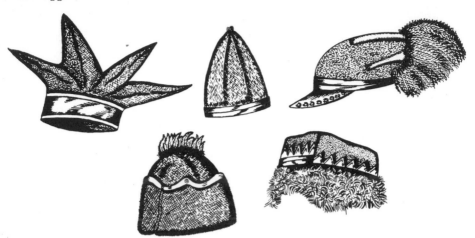

Fig. 40. Five types of male headgear. Top: left, Norwegian; centre, Central Swedish; right, North Swedish and Finnish-Lapp pattern. Bottom: left, Southern Swedish; right, from Kola peninsula region, USSR

Fig. 40

Lappish headgear is also full of character. All the way from Lake Inari in the east, over the rest of Lapland, we see the typical man's cap or beret. It has four points – in Scandinavia, it is nicknamed 'the beret of the four winds', – so that its wearer rather suggests a medieval court-jester. In some Norwegian zones these points are less emphasized. On the other hand, now and again you run into Lapps wearing caps with four great dangling horns. You would think they were trying to get as close as possible to a reindeer's antlers for their headgear – even trying to merge their very identity with the animals!

Fig. 40

In nearly all districts the cap is called a *gâpper*. The original version seems to have had only one point, and that simply formed by sewing the material round. The most primitive pattern to be seen today is that favoured by the nomadic groups of the Swedish Jokkmokk zone – though European types of hat are often seen too. The *gâpper* will often be given an ornamental touch in the form of coloured bands crowned by a bold button or pompom. Fashion, with its typical capacity for

Fig. 41. Three types of Lapp women's head-dress: left, Northern Swedish; centre, Central Swedish; right, Kola peninsula, USSR

caprice, seems to have decreed that an even larger bow shall be worn. The result is that from Gällivare to Torneträsk the Lapps come out with enormous red pompoms on their berets – so huge, in fact, that in rough weather it can be quite a problem to keep the beret on, especially when the pompom is drenched with rain into the bargain. Until a few years ago, this style was exclusive to the Karesuando Lapps of northern Sweden – so-called after a village in the district. But this group was forced southward into new territory when the closing of a frontier up in their old northern homeland put a stop to the migrations of their reindeer – and so, too, their own.

Swedish and Norwegian Lapps often wear caps with a peak. It is pierced with holes and reinforced with minute brass rings. It may also be decorated along the edge, particularly among the nomads of Könkämä, Lainiovuoma and Saarivuoma. Such decoration can be seen in the cap-peaks of the south too, but in a rather less rich and varied form.

Fig. 40

At Jukkasjärvi and Vittangi a note of austerity prevails. Clothes are plain, ornament reduced. Laestadius, the Lutheran pastor, is still the guiding spirit here. Even the indomitable red pompom has shrunk to the most modest dimensions.

Today Lapland has a tourist value, and this has unfortunately encouraged a minority of less sensible Lapps to exaggerations of local colour, with the result that the four horns and the red pompom dangle over the male brow. The Petsamo zone, however, and for the most part Russian Lapland, disdain this. The caps here are square in shape, fur-bordered, and for ornamentation, a few triangular embellishments are reckoned sufficient.

Fig. 41

The women – unlike those in most other parts of the world – put on less of a show. In Finland and in some Norwegian districts, they wear a veiled hat decked out very simply with a little white lace at the front. At Karesuando, a coloured ribbon going all the way round is the mode. The crown is flat and the ear-pieces carry a little lace-trimmed braiding. At Jukkasjärvi and a few other places, fashion decrees a pointed blue beret – but this is becoming rarer. The berets of Gällivare and Jokkmokk are worn with a pleat – at the back if the wearer is on the way home, at the front if she is going out. Lapp women of Härjedalen, in Sweden, which is a fair way south for Lapps to live, favour something in the nature of a cloth busby. It may have finishing touches at the front or the sides, or else it will carry some plaited coloured ribbon. Occasions of particular solemnity bring the men out in this style of hat also. An alternative male form here is a black silk beret, peaked like a cap. Sometimes it is tricked out with a startling red crest. Then there are parts of Lapland where the headgear of the male is derived – or at any rate, used to be – from the skin of a bird. The plumage was worn at the front and there was no lining.

Wet weather, in Norway and Sweden, brings out the Lapps in a cape called a *luk'kâ* in the north and a *skupmuk* in the south. It is made of heavy material, and may have had a predecessor of the same style in bear-skin. This garment gives protection to the back and the chest, and a collar keeps the icy wind out.

Cloth reaches the Lapps through ordinary commercial channels: reindeer pelts, obviously, they provide for themselves. The tanning process is interesting and follows ancient traditional methods.

The skins of the slaughtered reindeer are stretched, dried, and then kept in a dry place. Curing is delayed until the next spring. The women take the pelts and give them a week or two's good soak in water. They must be pliable enough to handle without danger of cracking. They are then boiled in a cauldron with strips of birch-bark – after the hair has been shaved off. A few days of this and the skins are as soft as they can be. A smoothing implement with a double scraper is then applied to them. The Lapps call it an *jiek'ko* and it is familiar to a number of Siberian peoples. After some hours of this treatment, which is very thorough, the skins are hung in a shaded place to dry out completely. But even then, the end of the complex process has not quite been reached. A dressing of flour and fish-oil is prepared by the women and applied liberally. It only remains to leave the skins heaped up together and let the mixture soak into the weighty pile.

It is the women who prepare the reindeer-skins. It is also part of the woman's sphere to turn the sinews into thread, string and binding, while the man makes the household utensils out of wood and horn. The Lapps, in the isolation of their vast tundra-lands, are kept busy continually. There are a thousand tasks to divide between man and woman and if they neglect them they cannot survive.

In many of the tents today there is a sewing machine, so that hand-sewing is needed only for garments made from reindeer skin – when it follows a traditional technique as old as the memory of man, a technique which has changed little from the days when the needles were made of bone. At one time the sole source of sewing thread was the reindeer's sinews. The manner in which it was prepared is described thus by Manker:[12] 'With her teeth and her fingers, the woman tears the sinews into thin fibres which she winds round her right hand. When these are ready she places them between her lips to keep them moist and "spins" them on her knee. Her apron is kept taut by being tucked tightly under her thighs and her right hand passes constantly up and down to roll the fibres into thread, while the left hand holds the end firmly. The ends of each length of fibre are frayed out between the teeth and they are rolled to, gether into a single thread, with no visible join. The finished strand is wound slowly round the middle finger, the ring, finger and the little finger of the left hand, the thumb and fore, finger being left free to hold the work taut. When the product is of sufficient length it is unwound and rolled on the knee again into a strong double, stranded thread.'

Lapp women are very old hands at plaiting. Their braiding and their ribbon, work have the stamp of real mastery. But their greatest skill comes out in their weaving: it is undoubtedly a skill which has been handed down from the earliest times. It has produced implements pertaining to Lappish culture and to no other – like the small loom on which the great majority of the work is done. This may be constructed in bone or in wood. It comprises a variable number of winders within a rectangular frame. Every winder has a hole at the centre. The threads are passed through these holes at tension, and then again through the gaps between one winder and the next. The woof is formed by shifting the winders and it can be varied in com, plexity with the lines they form.

Another ancient skill goes into the tin filigree work with which the Lapps decorate their reins. At one time it was also found on the little appendages of their magic shamans' drums.

Fig. 42

They obtain the wire with the aid of a *tatne,tjorve* – literally, a 'horn tool for tin'. Through it they pass very narrow tin strips, holding them tight with the teeth, and working them down as fine as possible.

But it is in their bone and horn carving that the Lapps can be considered past, masters. Here they have preserved almost without change all those characteristics of their heritage which derive from what is broadly termed the 'reindeer, age' or 'sub, Arctic culture'. Equally striking is their work on wood:

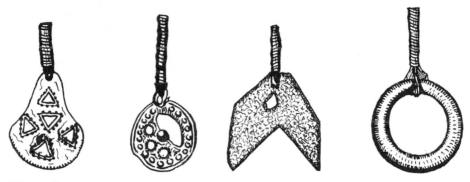

Fig. 42. Copper ornaments, attached to the edges of shamans' drums

pine for the under-part and the sides of their sleds, and for skis used on frozen snow; birch for skis to cope with softer snow, and for their milk buckets and the bowls of their pipes. Chisels and scraping-tools of many types are put to a variety of uses: in the Iron Age these were made of flint or quartz. The most characteristic is the *lokker*, which is quite primitive in design, comprising merely a piece of iron embedded in a neck of wood. Another instrument used for carving, with a circular blade, is the *sâha*.

The present-day Lapps who gain their means of sustenance exclusively from the raising and exploitation of reindeer are relatively few in number. They comprise groups in northern Norway and Finland, and also *sii'dâ* in the forests of the Vittangi area, approximately on the border between Sweden and Finland. A group with an economy of this kind is found even in the Gällivare area, more to the south, but this is a case of elements from Vittangi having subsequently migrated.

Apart from these, all Lapps keep other kinds of animals with them: goats, for instance, to provide milk and cheese. The nomadic mountain-Lapps very rarely drink reindeer milk, merely eat the meat in various forms. They get cereals, potatoes, dried fruits and butter from the villages.

The staple diet is reindeer meat – not one scrap of which is wasted. The flesh of the bear is the most prized reward of the hunt. Salmon and trout – above all, sea-trout – make the choicest fish dishes. Angelica, 'Icelandic' lichen, myrtle and other berries all add flavour to their food. The eggs of sea-birds, and those of inland species are greatly sought after.

Bread of a kind, without yeast, is made, though flour of course must be bought.

Water, milk and coffee are the commonest drinks. *Sjömar,* made from curdled milk reinforced with alcohol, has now largely disappeared. Spirit, which has ruined the health and the morale of whole populations, is nowadays seldom to be obtained by barter and no longer constitutes a threat.

THE LIFE OF THE SPIRIT

CHAPTER IX

The Supreme God and the Gods of Nature

THE LAPPS, WHEN DISCOVERED by a few roving merchants and priests from the outside world, had no single religion. They were a people of varying beliefs. But all of these sprang from the same ancient culture, all were born of the common mythology once shared throughout the sub-Arctic, and through them we can sometimes hear an echo from the proto-historic period and the dawn of civilization itself.

In the oldest Lapp legends that have come down to us, the Supreme Divinity was *Ibmel*. This was a Uranic god, and he remained an abstract idea, never given any concrete form in art. *Ibmel*, it is reasonably certain, was not an original Lappish conception. The Supreme God of the Finnish tribes, *Jumala*, was an identical figure. Perhaps there is a strong eastern influence at work here: the Cheremiss people has a very similar version too in its *Jume* – a word which in its Finno-Ugric tongue means 'sky'. Also, the name for the Uranic god of the Samoyeds, *Num*, means 'sky': the same root-ward is involved. The sun and moon are *Num*'s eyes.

We can be sure that before they came under the Finno-Ugrian influence (which is to be seen in their language of the present day) the Lapps worshipped the sun – *Bœi've*, in their present language. The sun-god was often depicted on the magic drums as a leading figure among lesser divinities. *Fig. 43*

We gather from a Lapp legend that *Ibmel*, after creating the earth, sent down to it *Māddâr-akko* – 'woman and mother' – to bring life. Is there an implication here of some mystic union of the sky and the earth? The myth of such a celestial marriage is notably absent among all Uralo-Altaic peoples, so this idea may spring from indigenous Lappish beliefs. The woman-figure as the life-giver has no place in Finno-Ugrian beliefs, though she appears in the Palaeo-Siberian and also in the extremely ancient and prehistoric culture of the Aurignacian and Magdalenian Ages.

The Supreme God goes largely unmentioned in Lappish belief. It may be that the reindeer-hunters turned away from the concept of a celestial being, a figure dimly connected with the beginning of things, and now entirely remote from the hard actualities of a created world. *Māddâr-akko,* on the other hand, is to this day a living symbol in race-memory. The tradition of ancient festivals held in her honour still lingers on – for instance, in the rites observed at a child's christening.

Fig. 43. Stylized representation of the sun: a painting on a Lappish drum

With all the Arctic peoples it is the same story. The Supreme God was set aside in favour of lesser gods. Sacrifices were made to him only when all else failed. This god was held to be an aloof figure, never given to active intervention in human affairs. Others, more involved with humanity, took his place. The Uranic god, it was felt, was static as opposed to man, the dynamic. Man had his being in life, he was conscious of his own life-force in himself and he was surrounded by further evidence of it in the animals and the plants. So the Uranic god was gradually forgotten. The gods to be remembered were those of Nature, who appeared to share man's harsh battle for existence. They alone could lay claim to man's regard. Man came to feel that he was no longer alone, but rather bound up with a single ageless process of development and growth. Here is a clue to the strength of the *Māddâr-akko* cults, and those of the other Nature-gods. With the Lapps they have never lost their influence, even after an eventual decline of the Uralo-Altaic culture.

Among the Nature-gods, we have mentioned *Bæi've,* the Sun: this cosmic being was represented in stylized form as ubiquitous fire-emitting, life-giving rays. The solar deity must definitely be compared with *Ibmel*; maybe he was originally the same god, who was worshipped to an equal extent by the people of the Arctic zone under various names. Thus, *Jumala* of the Finns, *Jume* of the Cheremiss people, *Num* of the Samoyeds, *Hamui* of the Ainu, all indicate 'the sky'. Elsewhere, among the Arctic peoples, we may note the addition of a name to indicate the personification of the god. In this way we get the *Num-Turem* 'Turem of the Sky' of the Voguls; the *Num-Senke* of the Ostyaks of the river Irtish, with the same meaning; though there is reversion, among other groups of Ostyaks, to the word *Jem* which means good.

On the other hand, the Lapps worshipped an anthropo-morphic god called *Ač'če,* 'the father', who produced the thunder; sometimes he was represented in the shape of a bird. Later he became identified, according to Scandinavian scholars, with Thor through contact with the world of Germanic mythology, under the name of *Tiermes*. It should be mentioned that the word *Ač'če* – which even appears in the Slavic *Otek* – appears to provide a connection with other Arctic and sub-Arctic peoples, and, surprisingly, with some groups of American Indians, situated farther south than in former times: the Pawnees for example, worshipped a Supreme Being to whom they gave the name of *Tirava Atius,* in which *Atius* stands for 'father'. His symbol, which was present in some religious ceremonies (for example, in the *Hako* ritual), was a bird's plume. Similarly, among the Cheyenni and the Arapako the god of thunder was represented by a bird.

Fig. 44. Biegg-Olbmai, *the Wind-divinity, as he appears on a drum*

Moreover, the word Tiermes evidently bears an affinity with the divinity of the Voguls and of the Ostyaks, *Torim* and *Turem,* with the *Tura* of the Ciuvaks, the *Tangra* of the Yakuts, the *Tangheri* of the Buriati, and the *Tenghere* of the Tartars; in all probability it spread southwards and eastwards, thus suggesting an association with the Chinese *Tien* and the *Tamoi* of some American Indians.

Fig. 44

No force of nature made a deeper impression on the Lapps than the wind, which blows across the Tundra with incredible fury. This wind, it was believed, was kept in a cave by *Biegg-Olbmai* 'The Man of the Wind', who would release it to race over mountain and marshes, as the whim took him. Only the shamans had power over the winds, but they first had to tie them in three knots, which was a tremendous feat even for a magician. *Biegg-Olbmai* was only placated when the ice melted in an early spring, and when the reindeer started to migrate towards the mountains. Free from the crust of ice, the plants became green again and tentatively put forth shoots, while over all the countryside blew the gentle breeze of *Rana-Nieida*, who carefully tended growing flowers and plants. *Rana-Nieida* was the daughter of *Ač'če* 'the father', who came to be called *Radien-Attje*, i.e. 'the father who commands', when he was appointed the first person in a trinity, and the founder of a fairly numerous family of minor divinities. This god had a consort, *Radien-Ak'ka*, 'the woman who commands' (the second person in the trinity, not to be confused with *Māddâr-akko*, the woman-creator), and a son, *Radien-Kiedde* 'son of him who commands', who was sometimes called *Coar've-Radien* (literally, 'he commands and has reindeer antlers'). The son of *Ač'če* is often represented in this way on the drums of the shamans. When the Lapps met with the first missionaries, they often identified or confounded the ancient Nature-gods with the figures of Christianity.

Fig. 45. Varalden-Olbmai, *the Earth-god, in a painting on a drum*

The moon, first called *Aske* and then *Mano*, the Indo-European word, was important in early times but later lost its place in the cult. In this respect, the Lapps are far removed from the Samoyeds who considered the moon as the evil eye of Num (the sun was the good one), and from other Siberian peoples who worshipped the moon as a fertility goddess. Over the earth presided *Varalden-Olbmai*, 'Earth-man', over the waters it was *Tjas-Olbmai*, 'Water-man'. Similarly, *Leib-Olbmai*,

Fig. 45

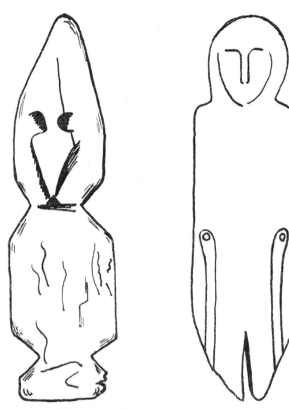

Fig. 46. Two carved figures, probably idols. The figure on the left, carved in wood, was discovered in the Mugi Forest, USSR, and is of Ostyak origin. It is now in the National Museum of Anthropology, Florence. The right-hand figure is of carved amber, and is prehistoric. It was found at Kurisches Haff, in the region of Schwarzort

'Blood-man', presided over wild animals and was eventually considered as the god of hunting who distributed game over his wide domains.

Some divinities took part in the process of human procreation. There was *Radien-Kiedde,* who gave to *Māddâr-akko* a spirit for safe-keeping. This *Māddâr-akko* sheltered within her body for a while, until it assumed bodily form. Then she gave this little being to one of her daughters, whom the Lapps called *Sar-Ak'ka*, 'the woman who spins'. The latter secreted herself under the hearth of the tent or hut, and found a way of transferring the child-about-to-be-born to the woman who lived there. All this happened under the vigilant watch of two other feminine divinities, *Uks-Ak'ka*, 'Door-woman', who watched over the entrance, and *Juks-Ak'ka*, 'woman of the bow' who would take the infant under her protection.

Plate 25

There were other divinities as well. The Lapps had images of them carved in wood which they used to set up in hidden places in the forest, and they used to build rough altars for them on which they held sacrifices. Francesco Negri, who visited Lapland in the second half of the seventeenth century, claims to have succeeded in seeing one of these very 'idols':

Plate 26

'I have seen it newly put together, with the altar and the offering. The altar is made of many adjacent pieces of wood of equal length supported by four others in the ground about half the height of a man; the idol was made out of a small (*bedollo*) tree, with branches and leaves covered over with earth, and the trunk rising out of it . . . On the altar was the offering in the form of a whole reindeer-antler attached to part of the skull; this they wore, when they pretended to have received the gift of happiness from the reindeer, and, with their families, they ate the meat from it.'

CHAPTER X

The Dwelling of the Dead

CHURCHES IN LAPLAND are few in number; they are scat-tered over an immense territory. Yet for many years past, whenever this has been humanly possible, the Lapps have carried their dead to the churchyard. However long the journey, the priest must be summoned to pray for the dead man's soul.

Even so there are times – in winter, or in the course of the spring migrations to new pasture-lands, or, again, if the bereaved are far off in the mountains – when church and priest are out of reach. If someone should die under such circum-stances, the Lapps will take down his tent, at the same time leaving the poles standing, and the fire alight in their midst. The smoke is now free to rise as high as it will over hill or tundra. When the fire is out, they will take up the poles and tie them to a reindeer's pack-saddle. Then they will bury their clansman, where the ashes have grown cold. Sometimes, if wood is easily to be had in the region (a rarity, though, at this latitude!) they will leave the tent-poles in the ground. So it may happen that a traveller among the mountains will come across the signs of an old fire surrounded by four wooden poles which are fighting a losing battle with time and with snow. If the traveller looks closely, he may also find a stone. Beneath it lies some Lapp nomad who has gone to join his forebears.

This practice of abandoning a habitation so soon after death has struck is one that has particularly deep roots in Russian Lapland. Behind it lies a profound and ancient fear: the dead used to be blamed for visiting grave ills upon the living. Whenever a severe calamity befell, the shaman was con-sulted. With his magic drum, he could tell which of the spirits of the departed was guilty of sowing the seeds of some sudden epidemic or causing some heavy family misfortune.

135

A Lapp mother will often appear to recover very quickly from the loss of a son, devoted as she may have been to him during his life-time and given over to despair by his death-bed. but the more nomadic the clan, the deeper goes the fear lest the dead bring some sort of doom on the living. It is this fear which holds sway over the most hearfelt grief.

In some parts of Lapland, the body of the deceased would be hoisted up into a tree. This is still the usage among certain Siberian peoples, for example, the Yakuts. Before the actual interment, which thus formed the second part of the funerary rite, the body must be exposed for a time to the elements.

Long ago, the Lapps practised strange rites when one of their number joined those spirits whose world lies beyond the tomb: that world which the Lapps knew as the kingdom of *jabmi-aimo*. Only the sparsest record of such rites now remains. It seems beyond doubt, however, that they often abandoned the dead where they fell, just as the Samoyeds of this day will leave their departed to the snow-covered tundra, or, if they should succumb in the short summer season, to the wolves and to the midges and mosquitoes that swarm about their poor remains. To abandon the dead in such fashion is the common custom of very nearly all Arctic peoples. In point of fact, we know of North American Indian tribes who will leave their fellow-men, when they are no more than mortally sick or wounded, to be-come a prey to the jackals and wolves that roam the great plains, and the huge carrion birds. Among the Eskimos and a number of North-East Asiatic races, it is the same.

Some seek to explain such behaviour on the part of these primitive peoples towards their dead and wounded in the following way. The voracious wolves of the Arctic strike terror into the hearts of the living, because the scent of blood will draw them across the widest distance: they seem able to smell out the presence of death. Cruel-seeming abandonment of kith and kin, then, may amount to nothing more than a defence-measure, casting no reflection on the feelings of the bereaved. In any case, the custom is by no means usual among all Lapps.

A Samoyed tribe – so we gather from the ancient chronicles – once used to ship all its dead to an island, called Vaigač, where there was a real cemetery. They put the body into a wooden coffin, dug out a shallow ditch, threw in the earth again, or the snow, and then sacrificed a reindeer whose skull they fixed on a stake. Slowly the island became a weird forest of tangled trees formed by the long, tortuous antlers rising from white and fleshless skulls.

Fig. 47. Drum-picture showing a reindeer carrying a dead man to jabmi-aimo, *the 'world beyond the tomb'*

Some of the more northerly Lapp clans also used to bury their dead in islets out in the lake, but they were careful to bury them deep. Others varied this usage slightly: when the lake was frozen, they would take their dead out by sled to an islet covered in snow. There they would abandon both body and 'coffin' – the sled on which it had been borne to its resting-place. Bodies have been found like that: skeletons, frozen stiff, laid out on a board between two runners. The reindeer for these island funerals were specially chosen. They had to be very docile, and both swift and sure of foot. White cloth was draped from their antlers to serve as funeral plumes. No one might stop the cortège or hinder its passage to the sacred islet where the ancestors, the *saivo-olmak*, or 'happy men', would have spent the night deciding the fate of this, the latest addition to their number. All the evidence points to the fact that here again it was this ancient fear of the dead that led to such burials. Left on a little tract of earth surrounded by water, the dead were powerless to rejoin the living in their tents. If it was

Fig. 47

winter, they were still cut off from them; for, once the reindeer had been unharnessed from the funeral sled, the dead could never make their way across the frozen lake to its shores. Their families could therefore rest in peace: no sudden evil could visit them from that quarter.

The people of the tundra have devised many methods of severing all links with their dead. The last rites are sometimes celebrated within a ring of fire. The departing mourners cross it, and they cannot be followed. But among some other Arctic races, this fear of the departed, with their propensity for bringing doom to the living, is even more exaggerated: is so intense indeed, that in certain parts of North-East Asia there is a powerful taboo on going to the help of anyone who falls into water; what is more, should he succeed in getting out again by his own efforts, no one will speak to him. He is treated exactly as if he were dead. In fact, one begins to wonder if death, among such peoples, is not really regarded as a sort of conta-gious disease. Why otherwise should a man be 'buried' before he has drawn his last breath?

The Lapps have many characteristics that are shared by their Arctic neighbours in general, but it must be borne in mind that they are never driven to excesses of this order. A Lapp whom some mishap has befallen can always rely on a helping hand from his neighbour, however grave his hurt, however much he may be in peril of his life.

Some Lappish groups – the Skolts for instance, who in-habit a frontier region between Finland and the USSR, – used to turn their dead into nothing less than divinities: they had no fear of them at all. When they saw the aurora borealis, they were convinced that they were watching a Dance of the Dead. The spirits of the departed, abandoning their tombs, had flown off towards the Arctic North. There, gathering at the highest point in the sky, they were weaving round one another in dance. This belief was rather at variance with that of certain Norwegian Lapps, who held the aurora to be a mirage of the sea.

In August 1945 at Tjalmejaure, in Svaipa district, Manker photographed a stone of a strange type, 2 feet 4 inches high. Plate 22 Local Lappish tradition claimed that it represented *Tjalto-kerke*. The idol had been removed fifty-three years before, and now had reappeared in its appointed place, which marked the site of an ancient encampment.

The fact is that the Lapps have never quite dropped the notion that a stone, even a small one, is capable of manifesta-tions which can reveal it in a terrifying light. A rock or a stone needed no exceptional proportions to assume power of which the Lapps felt quite in awe. There were stones borne aloft by ancient glaciers or mysteriously propelled to strange places in prehistoric times; there were meteorites plummeted down from the sky – an undeniable sign of some power beyond our world. Sacrifices were on occasion made to these stones; they claimed the finest reindeer of the herd. And as the animal's blood ran over the stone, the Lapps went down on their knees and fervently invoked the spirits of their ancestors.

It is now believed that what the Lapps saw in these stones, which they called *siei'de,* was a sign of the thraldom of those departed spirits who never gave them peace. Perhaps they had to atone for some guilt, and that was the motivating force which, from beyond the tomb, stole into some mute stone. The stone, indestructible, eternal, thus came to suggest a symbol of unending doom. The living sacrificed their reindeer in the hope that their propitiated gods would keep them free from the perils which the spirit-world had stored up for them.

A long, hard struggle with the elements has endowed the Lapps with a peculiarly sharp sensibility. It may well be by virtue of this that another tradition lingers stubbornly with them to this day – the notion that some stones are 'sacred'. At the root of this conception, as of so many others, lies that over-weening desire for peace – peace for themselves and for the dead. The churchyard offered them this peace, but only the acceptance of Our Lord could allow them to lie in its tran-quillity beneath the ancient forest pines. So now, after a life-time's wandering through valley and marsh, and a lifetime's puzzlement over the problems of existence and human destiny, the Lapps find their last resting-place in the shadow of the little churches scattered over the vast solitudes of their wild land.

CHAPTER XI

The Cult of the Bear

THE BEAR, IN LAPLAND, was hunted and killed with a ritual which is of the greatest interest to the student of this strange people.

The earliest missionaries, reaching their boundless northern forests between 1500 and 1600, found the ceremonial in full swing and in many districts, in spite of a total conversion to Christianity from the old pagan beliefs, it survives today.

The Lapps consider the bear to be the animal-king. This may be because he can stand up on his two hind-paws and strike attitudes which are almost human. Or again, the explanation may lie in an age-old traditional belief, which holds the bear to be an ancestor of the race. The Lapps claim for this animal the full intelligence of one man and the strength of nine men. How otherwise could the shamans, clad in his skins, visit any of the five heavens inhabited by the gods, as some nomadic clans believed?

According to the older generation, at any rate, a bear may be attacked by any number of men and he will not retreat – unless among the hunters there are two brothers. Then, they will tell you, he will flee. For he has some strange power to smell out two men of the same blood and he reasons that since one regards a brother's life as being as precious as one's own, the danger to a hunted animal is doubled, no man of good-will being likely to abandon a brother in danger.

This belief credits the bear with reasoning powers of a high order. Other Arctic peoples besides the Lapps: the Samoyeds, the Ainu, and other Siberian and North American races, see him in the same light. The bear was, moreover, once thought to enter into mystical relationships with the tribe. Sometimes he was regarded as an oracle – he could reveal, for instance, whether a coming child would be boy or girl. Lapp women were forbidden to hunt the bear, but they were said to be glad to meet one! Those who were pregnant would stop, hoping he would deign to give them a glance. If he growled, it meant the woman was carrying a son: if he 'smiled', it meant a daughter. In Lapland, however, especially in winter, men and women were dressed so much alike that the bear could scarcely be expected to tell the sex of the figure approaching him, leave alone that of a still unborn child. The women would help him out by giving a quick tug at their petticoats.

It may seem strange to us that this deep veneration for the bear did not prevent the Lapps from hunting him. They were compelled to do so by their hard life, and the fact that more than one family would find difficulty in obtaining sufficient food. The bear-hunt followed an elaborate ritual. It began with the searching out of the bear and did not come to an end until several days after the kill.

The various members of the hunting party would meet by the tents or huts dressed up in their brightest blue, beribboned with red and yellow, braceleted at wrist and arm-pit with their precious and sacred emblems. Then off they would go in silence, very careful not to pronounce the word 'bear' in case all their plans should go awry and the bear become enraged before the time was ripe: among nearly all primitive peoples, we find this superstition – speak the name of a spirit, or an animal, and there he is. The Lapps are no exception. At the most there would be affectionate references to the 'Old 'Un' or 'Old Forest-Apples' or 'Honey-Paws'. The hunted beast could be expected to put up a good fight, but he was conquered in the end. The Lapps had devised a method of dispatching him by which everyone was exonerated from having struck the fatal blow. They would plan their assault for the time when the animal was just coming out of his winter sleep, but was still in his den; namely, March or April. That den will have been marked out some days earlier, by means of a circle traced round it in the snow. These 'rings' denoted possession by the finder, and in some districts there was quite a trade in them.

An advance-guard of bold spirits would slip into the den. The animal, angered at last by these intrusions, would scramble out to bowl down his assailants. But lying in wait for him there were a host of *sai'te* – long, sharp, iron-tipped spears, firmly planted at such an angle that they would pierce the beast as he plunged forward.

The wisest of animals having been dispatched by a trick, the hunters went down on their knees and asked his pardon for having killed him. If they were all unharmed, they offered him thanks for sparing them. But they were not allowed to touch him yet awhile. At a sign from the hunt-leader, they rose with a paean of joy and thanks on their lips. Then, singing still, they would return to the encampment.

Back there, from the moment when they had heard that distant cry of triumph, the women would have been preparing their age-old welcome. Their faces smeared with a reddish paste obtained by chewing birch-bark, they too would be singing in chorus. The songs they sang went by various names among the Lapps, but they were largely a matter of improvisa-tion – like the famous *juoigos* airs of which a considerable col-lection was made by Armas Launis some fifty years ago. (This collection was representative of Norwegian and Finnish Lap-land: songs of the Swedish Lapps were collected by Karl Tiren.)[1] On occasions such as this – the return of the men-folk from a bearhunt – the songs may have been versions of extremely ancient chants, all inspired by the bear-myth. To this day some Lapps claim that they were sung in a secret tongue: could this have been the original pre-Finnish language?

The homeward march of the men was headed by the hunter who had first traced the animal to this particular lair. He carried the spear on which the bear had impaled himself. On its tip there was now a magic ring, generally a brass one. As the men reached the camp, the women fell suddenly silent. Only the dogs which had taken part in the hunt made any noise at all. They would still be barking excitedly. And then followed a ritual that had all the implication of a re-birth and purification myth. In fact, if the Lapps looked on the bear as a wild being strangely linked with the tribe – something very close to a re-incarnated ancestor – now that they had killed him, they became actual physical participants in his death. The whole community's survival was therefore endangered. Purification must be sought.

On their return to the camp, the hunters would enter their respective tents, not by the accustomed tent-flaps but from the opposite side: they would crawl in under the skins behind the *boaš'šo*. The women, however, would enter in the usual fashion. Coming face to face with their menfolk, they would take off their caps. The men would now bow their bared heads, to receive the birch-bark spittle which the women were rolling round their mouths. The dogs also had their heads spat on and were then fastened to the tent-poles by brass chains.

What explanation lies behind this rite? What significance can we attach to the colour-factor – the red paste the women smeared over their faces, the red spittle which they spat at the men and the dogs? I can only think that this practice goes back to the time when Northern European hunters used to sprinkle a fallen companion with red ochre. By giving this colour to the dead man, they sought to restore life. We know that in some countries the custom lasted until the end of the Bronze Age. In Northern Russia – for a long time the home of the reindeer-hunters following the retreating ice – it was very widespread and lasted longer than anywhere else. If we are indeed dealing here with some latter-day relic of ancient observances, the implication of the red birch-bark paste would seem clear enough. The hunters had killed an animal with whom they felt themselves to be strangely linked; therefore they themselves had been touched by death. The moment when this happened was the moment of the kill, and it was marked by their cries of triumph. The women left at home heard these cries. They felt that in so far as death had now touched their menfolk, it had brushed by them too. That is why at this precise moment they smeared their faces with red. This was a rite of re-birth. Having performed it, they re-entered the tent, in the accustomed manner. To the men, their women as they waited to greet them at the hearth-stone were in a manner of speaking a personification of the creative goddess *Māddâr-akko*. Now *Māddâr-akko*, through her daughter *Sar-Ak'ka* – who lived beneath the hearth stone – was empowered to give life. For this boon the men stood bare-headed. Their women-folk renewed their life by spitting the colour of life on their heads. The dogs, boon-companions of these men of the north, came in for the same treatment.

The significance of the next stage of the ritual is difficult to explain. The women looked at the men through little rings of polished brass, all the while backing towards the tent-flap by which they sought to leave. These rings were the ones which had been placed on the lances of those hunters who had first got on to the track of the bear. Had they some analogical relationship to the ring traced round the bear's lair to establish hunting rights? Or might they be sexual symbols, such as many primitive peoples used? The circle and the lozenge were shapes that characterized amulets often worn as a protection against sterility, or death.

Next morning, after the hunters had brought the dead bear safely into the camp, the ceremonial of the previous day was repeated. Thereafter, the festivities began. Everyone ate his fill, though care had to be taken not to break one single bone of the skeleton, for which a grave was finally dug. A man was

K

stationed by it to pronounce these words: 'With the coming of next spring, you will rise again, will roam the hills and sleep in a bed of myrtles. Pardon us now, forget that we have killed you. Yet we did not kill you. It was the arms carried by our hands.'

For a whole year, no woman was allowed to travel in the sled the bear had been loaded into. If she did this, she would become sterile – clear evidence of a bear-man relationship.

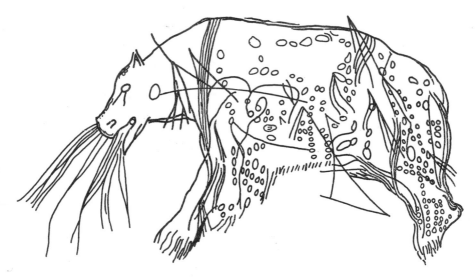

Fig. 48. Wounded bear; a prehistoric cave-painting at Les Trois Frères, Ariège, France

Even the reindeer drawing this sled was reckoned to have come under the spell of the bear. The women were forbidden to ride behind that particular animal, again for a whole year. A taboo not altogether dissimilar was placed on the hunters themselves: for three days they were not to consort with their wives – five days in the case of the man whose lance was the one on which the bear had actually impaled itself. The killing was

Fig. 49. Two representations of a bear: left, a Lappish drum picture; right, a rock-carving discovered at Finnhag in Afjord, Norway

clearly believed to be able to exert a baleful influence on the woman's reproductive faculties.

Siberian hunters likewise would not touch the bear after the kill. They danced round him, wearing masks of tree-bark or carved wood. The same practice was at one time adopted by the Lappish shamans. Striking proof that such rites were widespread is provided by cave drawings at Lascaux and the Trois Frères cave at Ariège in the Pyrenees. In the one, a witch-figure in red and black dances, masked and horned, in the midst of animals; in the other, the masked figure is wholly black. This was the sort of dance that was performed in the bear's honour. The bear himself is shown in the Trois Frères graffiti.

Fig. 9

CHAPTER XII

Shamans and Drums

IN ANCIENT TIMES, and to a progressively diminishing extent right up to the end of the last century, a strange ceremonial preceded the bear-hunt. One man had the all-important role of ensuring its success. This was the shaman – to use the Lapp word, the *noaï'de*. Squatting down before his tent he would beat a drum of strange pattern – a symbol which has played an outstanding part in the history of Lappish culture. The shaman was a man who had entered into relationship with the spirits – or else he was possessed by them. The Lapps turned to him in order that harmony might be established between the spirits and the real world. The shaman, in brief, was the intermediary between man and his gods.

We are unable to tell at what date the Lapps began to resort to the drum for purposes of divination or for communication with spirits and divinities. We only know that about the year 1500, the missionaries were hot on the trail of such cultural objects which they sought to consign to the flames as vehicles of sin and perdition.

Until that time, so far from the drum having belonged to the sphere of the shaman and no one else, it may well have been that every head of a family had his own, and could interpret for himself the magical signs and drawings executed on it. But until 1500 or thereabouts, we have no record of drums, and archaeological excavation and research have disclosed no trace of them. The question we have to decide therefore is whether we are dealing here with a branch of the magic cult which reached Lapland comparatively late, by way of Asiatic races of shamanistic religious beliefs; or with something rooted in the propitiatory rites which in Europe, right back to the Middle Palæolithic Age, accompanied the hunt.

We are certainly rather in the dark here. Not only are archaeological discoveries not forthcoming, but the ancient writers on Lapland are silent on the subject.

The magic drum is found among Arctic hunting-peoples spread out over a wide area – more especially those of Siberia and North America. In these regions, plenty have survived and we are at once struck by the very strong resemblance of the Altaic (North-Central Asian) drum to the Lappish pattern.

This can be divided into four distinct types according to the frame. It may be fashioned from a single strip of wood, pliable enough to be bent right round; from a natural circle of wood – a rarer variety; from two semi-circular pieces; or lastly, it may be a cup-shaped frame – more common, perhaps, in Norway and Sweden than elsewhere.

The first type, in common with the second, is found only in the more southerly regions of Swedish Lapland. The third – the frame formed of two halves – used to be made in the eastern parts of Finland, that is, the Lake Inari district towards the Kola peninsula. In Finland the drum was known as the *kannus,* while elsewhere the term used – applying as it did to drums having a frame all in one piece – was *gievre,* meaning, very aptly, 'ring'. The cup-shaped drum was called the *kobdes.*

This last variety had two hand-grips carved in the base. The others were fitted with a little handle. The skin used for these drums was that of a very young reindeer, and on it were painted signs and figures representing the forces of nature, and hunting-scenes. The missionary Knud Leem recognized, in addition, on the skins of these drums, the runic symbols brought by the Gothic inhabitants of southern Sweden from the East. These runes, to use the Saxon word (which means 'mystery' or 'secret'), were a kind of insignia forming an alphabet. Runes crossed Dacia, Pannonia, and Germania, to be next found beyond the Baltic on Scandinavian soil. The characters were painted on tombstones or monuments, or else carved into them.

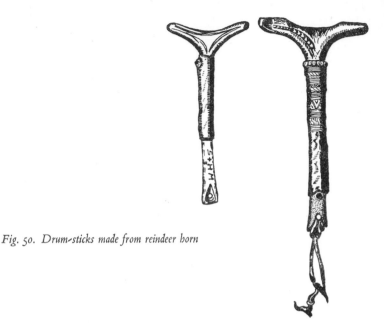

Fig. 50. Drum-sticks made from reindeer horn

The Swedish linguist Agrell discovered that they were also used in connection with magic, and with ritual: every rune had a numerical value bearing some relation to the various spirits of the water and the subterranean regions, and of the departed.

For beating his drum the shaman used a little stick or baton with a curved prong, made from reindeer horn and called a *vetjer*. It bore a striking resemblance to some of the so-called 'batons of command' found at Palæolithic level at Arene Candide in Liguria; in the Basses-Pyrénées; in the Dordogne; at Ariège, and other places.

A piece of wood or a ring was placed ready on the tightly stretched skin. When the drum was beaten it jumped about over the magic signs and figures. The shaman would suddenly break off. From the sign at which the ring or the piece of wood had come to rest, he would cast the auguries. The little 'dice' was called the *arpa*. According to Manker, in some regions it was identified with a jumping frog.

The surface of these drums, then, depicted divinities and hunting and fishing scenes – aspects of daily life. The sun-god *Bæi've* was often found, symbolized by a circle or rhomboid form from which darted long rays. Above were other divinities, such as the God of Thunder or the 'Man of the Winds', *Biegg-Olbmai*. Sometimes, especially in drums of the Nordic type, the skin was divided into a number of parts – up to five – by which the artist sought to represent the divisions of the universe. In addition to the trinity formed by *Radien-Ač'če, Radien-Ak'ka* and *Radien-Kedde,* portrayed on the upper part of the skin, there were a good many others: the mythological world of the Lapps was a well-populated one. We find *Uks-Ak'ka,* pro-tectress of the hut-door; *Juks-Ak'ka,* the woman of the bow and guardian of the children; a figure on horseback called *Rota,* representing death – this divinity came very much under the the influence of Germanic myth and has sometimes been identified with Odin; *Māddár-akko* was painted on the drums too, though not in the place of honour, which was reserved for *Bæi've.* All these figures were sharply divided from one another: they were virtually in separate squares, so to speak, so that when the *arpa* came to rest as the drumbeats ceased, there should be no confusion over which figure it had stopped at.

Fig. 51. *A shaman with his sacred drum*

The skin also contained drawings of a whole host of men, clearly indicated in the role of hunter, fisherman or shaman. The animal kingdom was represented too, often by the reindeer, the elk, the wolf, the bear and the badger. There were also fish and birds. On some drums, the Lappish dwelling was depicted – hut, reindeer-pen, *njâllâ* and all, even the bow and arrow and the sacrificial altar.

Fig. 51

Indeed, it is a picture of the entire Lapp world that comes to life on these drums. Their importance to the student is immense. Manker, from whose works we have already quoted, has become the leading authority on the rich material they offer, and all those interested in the cultural evolution of this Arctic

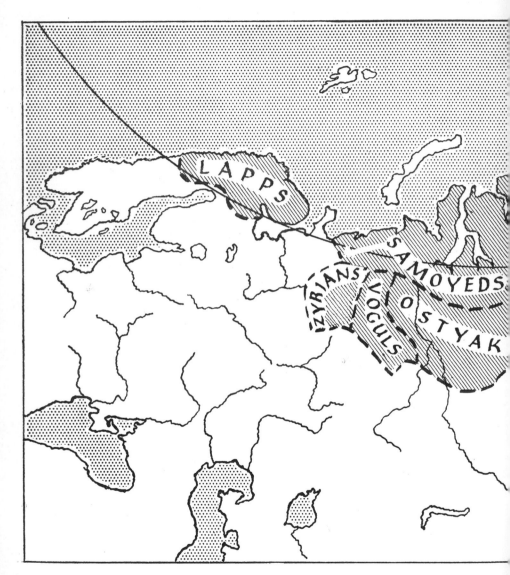

Fig. 52. Map showing regions occupied by the Arctic peoples of Eurasia.

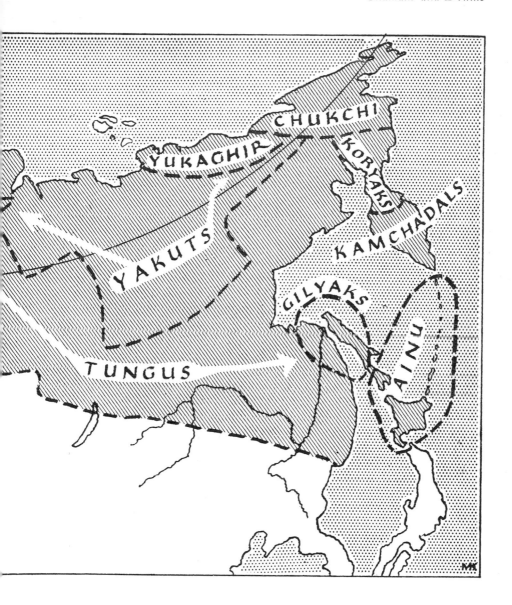

people stand deeply in the debt of this pioneering Swedish ethnologist. Artistically, too, the drawings on the drums repay study, for they represent a halfway stage between a Palæolithic naturalism and the stylized simplifications of the Bronze Age. The little figures, painted in red, are at times highly stylized, but very rarely are they divested of a sense of life and movement, and this gives them a striking affinity with the scenes painted by Palæolithic man. For example, reindeer are never portrayed in a static attitude: the impression we gain is that the artist has tried to seize upon the dynamic quality so peculiar to this creature. He has really watched the animal in movement before setting to work.

The interpretation of the drawings, however, is not easy. We only know that the shaman established some relation between them and the forces of nature – themselves personified on the drums in the divinity-images – and then based his prophecies on the caprice of the *arpa*.

The function of the shaman among the Lapps links up again with the cults practised in the whole of North Asia by the nomadic tribes of stock-breeders, and has many points of contact with the religious rites of the Eskimo tribes, among them, in particular, the Ahiarmiut, the Iglulik and the Angekok, and with the most ancient customs of some groups of North American Indians.

It was inevitable that the shamanistic cult, with all the complexities of its prophecies and its invocatory rites, should call for a specialized category among the ancient Lappish people. Its devotees needed to be psychologically adapted for the vocation in the first place. They then had to be specially trained, and the office was given to those who had served the novitiate.

The first steps to the priesthood were simple enough. On some silent summer's night, a boy might have a strange dream in which he heard the voices of the Spirits. When morning came he told his father. The father, overjoyed, took him along

Fig. 53, 54

Fig. 53. Two reindeer as they appear on a drum: above, a big male; below, a sled-animal drawing a canoe-shaped sled

to the shaman, who learned that a sign from the gods had come to the boy as he slept. The boy turned to the old shaman with a word of greeting which showed a proper respect towards one who stood so high in the esteem of the clan: whereupon the father left his son to the care of the sacred tent.

Fig. 54. Two skiers depicted in drum-paintings

The first thing to be impressed upon the youngster was that one part of himself could achieve liberation during sleep, and that he must hold this spiritual side in awe. Then he was made to learn by heart phrases emphasizing the fragile nature of the body and the great power of the spirit. The boy learned how the first hunter had been created by *Ibmel,* and his sons made flesh-and-blood in the Woman-and-Creator, *Māddâr-akko* – who with the aid of her daughter made them pass into the bodies of Lapp women. The Lapps seem to have held that every living body was an integral part of the body of the Creative Being – a part that must ever be constituted anew, so that fresh generations of men could spring up.

A young novice in the shaman's care could be depended upon to possess a marked leaning towards onirism – that is, morbid dreams followed by hallucinations, and by mimetism. He would be specially subject to that 'Arctic hysteria' which would appear to be brought on by the driving winds and the ever-recurring snowstorms of the north, and perhaps also by the deepening numbness of the mind caused by long periods of immobilization.

Here was the raw material of the shaman's make-up. It only needed refining by means of instruction, solitude, fasting, exciting spirits or narcotics, dance and physical duress. Shamans under instruction soon came to wear an ascetic look. They lived lonely lives and once they had acquired the arts of divination, their own need of its excitement would keep them relentlessly rolling the drums.

The shaman beats his drum to attain a state of spiritual exaltation – beseeching the Godhead to enter into him, to cast him into a state of contemplative ecstasy. After a while he starts foaming at the mouth; he emits terrible groans. Sometimes he is the victim of spasms during which he seems to be struggling with implacable enemies. But then follows a state of absolute calm and unconsciousness, lasting for a whole day. When the *vis magica* has passed, in an atmosphere heavy with things that are not of the everyday world, the shaman starts speaking.

Now, no one dare touch the sacred drum and all is still, save for the distant rolling of some neighbouring shaman's drum. Our shaman will foretell the run of the bear-hunt, he will tell the listening throng what the rest of the hunting will be like, and what the fishing-prospects are; whether the winter that is now closing in will bring much snow; whether the reindeer, at the melting of the ice, will all calve; whether sickness will decimate the tribe and which of the recent dead must be blamed for dire happenings.

In Lapland, as in Siberia and North America, shamans won fame for their powers of so-called 'remote communication' – achieved when they were in a state of excitement after rolling their drums. It might happen that one of them was sitting quietly by his tent when for no apparent reason he would raise his head. Members of a watching group would see him listening intently, for all the world as if he had heard a voice calling him from far away. Then he would get up and start off in a certain direction, without turning to left or right, marching forward with his steps seemingly guided by some superhuman force. From that moment on, there was no stopping him until he had made a long journey, and in the course of it he would neither eat nor drink. Then, as suddenly as he had started off he would come to a halt, murmuring words which no one understood. This would be followed by a state of unconsciousness. At the end of the trance he might declare to those who had followed him on his journey that in such-and-such a village district, many miles off, men had died from a strange disease, or that a herd of wild reindeer or a family of bears were descending upon the encampment. And the men of his clan had ample chance to prove the truth of such assertions.

The missionaries of three centuries ago, pushing onwards as far as the northern-most fjords of Norwegian Finnmark, were the first to give us an account of the shamans and their sessions and the rites they performed, up on the mountains or in some forest glade. It is also to them that we owe what record we possess of the ancient Lappish legends.

CHAPTER XIII

Some Lapp Legends

THE TWO BROTHERS

THE LAPPS SAY THAT in the beginning *Ibmel*, the God of gods, created two brothers. They lived together in a land of mountain and marsh. Winter was not too severe. Then came the first snowstorm, threatening to bury the two men. One of them quickly made up his mind what to do. He found a cavern on the side of a mountain, and hid there till the storm was over. But his brother stayed where he was in the open, fighting grimly for survival. He won his battle. From him sprang the Lapps, choosing for their land the coldest on earth. But the one who sought shelter was the ancestor of the Men of the South; particularly – a Lapp will add, with a humorous twinkle – the Swedes.

THE ULDA

Not only were there evil spirits in the world. There were the Ulda too. In some parts they were known as the *Halde*. They were good at heart, and were thoughtful towards bears when they had fallen into their winter sleep: they kept them supplied with fresh food. The Ulda lived in some underground regions and in lakes that were *saivo* – happy. The Lapps declare that every place which forms a paradise for those who have passed on is *saivo*. The Ulda rode on sleds drawn by white reindeer jingling with a thousand silver bells and they were followed by a pack of hounds that never stopped howling: especially at night, when should anyone their mistresses not care for happen to be encamped on the surface just overhead, they made a truly terrible din. The humans the Ulda really liked were those with black hair and wagging tongues. And once upon a time, so the tale goes, these Ulda climbed up out of the bowels of the earth, hied to the nearest Lappish camp – and took away the children, leaving their own (rather ugly little creatures, to tell the truth) in exchange.

Morning came. The Lapp mother saw what a trick she had been played. What was she to do? She plucked some juniper-branches and gave the little new-comers a whipping. Now, not even the Ulda women could stop their ears to the piteous cries of their own flesh-and-blood, so they gave up their stolen children. But from that time forward, just to be on the safe side, a Lapp mother would hang a knife by her little son's cradle – or a needle by her daughter's.

The Chukchi have tales like that too – and they are a people living in the extreme north-east of Siberia. Their subterranean beings, however, are a kind of mice. They have reindeer, and sleds made of grass. Unlike the Ulda, they go bear-hunting. But they have one feature in common with their underground Lappish cousins: they are closely linked with the shaman. They appear to him in dreams. They see to it that he is well versed in his magic lore and whisper into his ear secret cures for the sick. The shaman can learn a lot from them: how to roll his sacred drum, how to choose his medicinal herbs, how to be a weather prophet, how to judge the chances of the hunt and where to find good lichen-grazing when out on migration.

Some Ulda, as we have said, inhabited mountain-lakes, and we are bound to add that these particular sprites – for that is what they were, just another version of the sprites and gnomes to be found in more than one people's folk-lore – were very fussy and irritable little beings, just the kind to say – 'Do so-and-so – or I'll pay you out!' Fishermen, for instance, plying the placid lakes of the north-lands, had to drop a coin into the water in order to get into the Uldas' good graces. For there they were, down in the depths, and they could prevent you from making a good catch if they had mind to. Eventually quite a lot of little pieces of money, *öre*, collected on the lake bed. The Ulda were pleased. And in that frame of mind they might even do a human being a favour. They might whisper to a mother-to-be – or to her shaman – the best name to give the new-born child. One famous legend had it that they could make you rich.

Often, in the silence of the night, the reindeer herdsman can hear the hoof-beats of the Ulda's herds passing beneath some slope. Throw a piece of iron in their direction – or so they say – and the reindeer will become real reindeer, of which the thrower may gain possession.

One day a Lapp met a young woman in the mountains, and she seemed so fair that on an impulse he took out his knife and threw it over his shoulder. The girl became his and he married her. He taught her to speak his tongue. When she had mastered it, she told him she stood to receive a great inheritance, and persuaded him to go to a place where he might set eyes on it. There were conditions, however. The young man had to lie with his head in her lap, keep his eyes shut and try and go to sleep. All this he did. After a little while, he heard a mighty thunder of reindeer hooves, and he opened his eyes. The herd was so vast that he could not see where it ended. But in that same instant, it was borne in upon him that if such riches were to be his, he would always have to obey his wife and do nothing except by her command. And he felt himself doomed.

STALO THE GIANT

Of all the monsters and the giants that dwelt in Lapland's far forests, the mightiest and the most formidable was Stalo. His wife was Lutakis the Treacherous. From her shoulders hung a birch-bark cradle, and in it were some horrible little brats of children. We learn from legend that the young members of this family had one eye in the middle of the brow. This was the only feature that set them apart from normal Lapp children. Yet

Stalo sent very few shudders down the spines of the Lapps. In the old stories, indeed, they are always making fun of him. But Stalo served one useful purpose—he was something to threaten naughty children with: he was the old, old ogre who kept his eye on every single thing a child did – and could spring out from nowhere whenever it suited him. The Lapps would tell their children that Stalo and Lutakis – Rutagis in some parts – were not only eaters of lizards, they were also kidnappers of young people, whom they shut up in pens like reindeer.

Every time they left a camping-ground – pooh-pooh him as they might – the Lapps took very good care to leave Stalo some water. Then the ogre would stop and drink, and this hindered him from catching up with the families who were migrating with the reindeer. In some regions of Sweden, they used to hint that Stalo found the human brain a very tasty morsel. He and his wife always did a great deal of coming and going round about Christmas-time, when he was particularly on the look-out for a young man to kill.

One day the giant found himself watching some Lapp children skiing down a hill. Wicked thoughts at once came into his mind. He got hold of some nets and made a trap to catch the youngsters. But their father was a Lapp with an eye so sharp it missed nothing, and he saw Stalo busy at his work. He guessed what mischief the monster was up to and without a second's hesitation plunged into the nearest marsh.

Having thus given himself a proper soaking, he allowed himself to be caught in the nets which Stalo had intended as a snare for his children.

The giant had hidden behind some birches, from which he now darted, to find his net full of moving flecks of colour. It was the victim struggling, in his bright Lapp clothes. But by the time Stalo actually reached the trap, his catch was frozen stiff. Triumphantly Stalo took him out of the net and carried him to his hut, where his wife was cooking supper.

L

Lutakis took hold of the Lapp and hung him over the fire to melt. Stalo set about looking for a saucepan to cook him in. Meanwhile his son noticed a strange thing. The Lapp was recovering; he was moving his eyes, and stirring. He called to his mother. Suddenly, however, the Lapp slipped the cord he was hanging by, and smote the son of Stalo on the head, felling him. Then it was his mother's turn. And in the middle of all the uproar, in came Stalo – to be blinded by boiling water from a cauldron. The Lapp now had no difficulty in dispatching the giant too, after which he returned safe and sound to his own tent.

THE BLINDING OF STALO

There are variants to this story of the blinding of Stalo which recall the Homeric tale of the blinding of Polyphemus by Odysseus. Here is one of the better known:

A young Lapp, lost in a pathless forest, happened upon the hut where the giant Stalo lived. Stalo made him welcome, and bade him sit down by the fire. Soon, however, the Lapp became aware of a savage look in the giant's eye. Forewarned is forearmed, and the guest suddenly thought of a plan.

'If I look into the fire,' he said, 'I see gold and silver.'

Stalo was astonished. He asked the other to substantiate this strange claim.

'Nothing so strange about it,' the Lapp replied. 'Anybody can see what I see. All he has to do is put a bit of lead in his eye'.

'Is that what you've done?' asked Stalo.

'Yes, of course,' said the cunning young Lapp.

Stalo thought for a minute. Then he rejoined, 'You ought to put a bit of lead in my eyes.'

The young Lapp asked him to lie down. Then, after he had melted some lead, he poured it into the giant's eyes. Stalo howled and squealed and the earth shook under him. As he got up, he realized that he was completely blind. Not only could he see no gold and silver, he could see no fire! He tried to seize the Lapp but of course the Lapp had no difficulty in slipping through his fingers. Then Stalo thought that the time had come for him to show a little cunning in his turn.

'Turn the goats out,' he said, taking up his stand by the door with his legs apart.

The Lapp gave the goats a push in the right direction. To go out of the cabin, the goats had to pass by the giant one by one and Stalo ran his hands over them as they went.

'Now the billy,' he commanded.

While the last of the goats were trooping out, the Lapp killed the billy-goat and put on his skin. On all fours he crawled between the giant's legs.

'Fine,' said the giant. 'Now you come too.'

But the young man was already outside the cabin and called out gleefully, 'I've already come.' Stalo was beaten. Only his sons, it seemed to him, could now get the better of this cunning guest. He asked the Lapp to tell him his name.

'Certainly I'll tell you,' said the Lapp. 'My name is I My-self.' As he said this, he fled. When Stalo's sons came in, they saw that their beloved billy-goat was dead.

'Who killed our billy-goat?' they asked angrily.

'I Myself,' Stalo replied.

Whereupon he himself was set on by his sons and killed.

Part Four

WHO ARE THE LAPPS?

CHAPTER XIV

The Problem of Lappish Origins

UNTIL RECENTLY, the Lapps were accepted as being of Mongolian origin. All the more accredited theories were adduced in support of this school of thought, and ethnologists still point to racial characteristics in its favour. But today's view is that their arguments are far from irrefutable: indeed, in the light of recent knowledge we may perhaps advance the claim that the Lapps are not only one of the most ancient races in existence, but that they stem from the great branch of primary Northern European races. Let us examine the evidence.

Linnæus may be considered to be the first student of Lappish origins. In his *Iter Lapponicum*[1] he claimed to have made a detailed study of his northern countrymen, and, as a result, to have discovered nothing in common between them and any other group. Being a frequent visitor at the encampments and an ever-welcome friend in many families, he had every chance to observe the Lapps at first hand. He has left us, as well as a book about his travels, a portrait of himself in Lappish costume – reindeer pelts – with a sacred drum attached to his belt. The illustrations in his book are also of great interest. They give us accurate information about many Lappish customs and traditions. Linnæus unfortunately did not pursue his Lappish studies for very long, having in the meantime undertaken his great work on the systematization of natural history on which his real fame rests.

Only seventy years later, however, the question was taken up again by Johann Blumenbach, the German naturalist. In a book published in 1804,[2] he divided the peoples of our globe into five principal races; in the second group, under the heading 'Mongolian Varieties', he put the Lapps, together

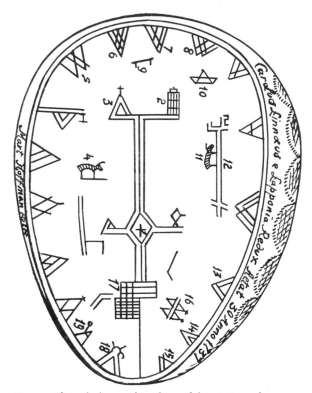

Fig. 55. Shaman's drum with markings of the animistic cult

with the Finns and the Palæo-Asiatics. This was to cause many a bitter dispute. But the official science of the day at first paid no heed to Blumenbach's pronouncements and made no attempt to pursue his lines of anthropological inquiry.

The theory of an eastern origin for the Lapps was all the surer of acceptance for having a certain romantic appeal. Thus, many years later, in 1886, the Swede Sven Nilsson starts off by stressing common somatic characteristics (less self-evident, perhaps, than he would have us suppose) and proceeds to prove that the northern nomads must have originated from a land east of the Urals – presumably the Altai valleys of Central Asia.[3] This would have meant an immense trek over steppe, tundra and mountains. But Nilsson's theory is that they made the migration and appeared in Europe about the time when the ice was receding. Towards the end of the last Ice Age, however, a race we may call 'Palæo-Arctic' already lived on the borders of the glaciation, and in all probability they came from the more southerly regions of the continent they already inhabited – Europe. It would have been interesting, in this connection, to examine any racial links between our reindeer-hunters and certain isolated ethnic groups which remained intact on approximately the line representing the original limit of the glaciation. In point of fact, the western Carpathians, the Black Forest, some regions of the Massif Central in France and the Swiss Oberland contain outcrops of extremely ancient races – the 'Alpine type', as they are now collectively called.

In all these regions archaeologists have found traces of a reindeer-hunting culture. But in 1886, anthropological inquiry proceeded along any lines but these.

At one point it was held that the Lapps were not a well preserved racial type: it was the vogue to describe them as a people who had entered the stage of pathological degeneracy. R. Virchow of Berlin came to this conclusion after examining a group of Lapps in 1875. 'They are thin,' he wrote, 'and have so many wrinkles, especially on the face, that the young men look quite old. By reason of a thin adipose tissue the skin has a fine texture quite rare in other European faces. In the region of the mouth particularly, where among other races men no less than women possess considerable adipose tissue, the skin of a Lapp is creased up like an old post-card. It seems to me that long periods of defective and inadequate nutrition will have had analogous effects on the entire organism, with the result that the Lapps may be considered racially a pathological example. . . .'[4]

Other writers supported this view. Yet it was no easy matter to substantiate the theory that the Lapps are the degenerate descendants of some original stock, when for at least 5000 years – the figure is a modest estimate – they had continued to exist in the harshest conditions man can endure.

Then it occurred to someone that they might be the descen⁄dants of the hunters following the retreating ice of the Würm glaciation – and the problem was at once simplified. The English authority Keane, the German Welker and others still clung to their belief in an eastern origin for the Lapps. Nor was this disapproved. Some held that those ancient reindeer⁄hunters who had migrated from the south became the Samoyeds, and not the Lapps at all; and the latter were reduced to a Samoyedic tribe which in remote times had drifted westwards, away from the original group. There were those who made the Urals responsible for this break⁄off of a splinter⁄group. But all their research was powerless to prove anything positive. The Samoyeds belong without any doubt to a pre⁄Mongoloid stock which received an admixture of purely Mongolian elements.

Moreover, Julius Kollman[5] noted in the Samoyeds such features as a wide face, slanting eyes and an extremely flat nose – a nose that is sometimes almost non⁄existent except in the lower region where the nostrils are situated. The adipose tissue continued right up into the lower eye⁄lid, giving the face a swollen look. This was very far from the typical Lappish appearance. In addition, Lapps have brown hair, tending to black; the Samoyeds have shiny black hair.[6] Nor could a Samoyed origin be proved for the old Lappish language.

The Frenchman Paul Topinard arrived at some striking results in the course of some anthropological investigations conducted using a special method: he noted and tabulated the combinations of height, skin⁄colour, nasal and cephalic characteristics. Classified thus, the Lapps became members of

a white race-group – the short-statured brachycephalic Lep-
torians, – and an ancient nucleus of Sardo-Ligurians was
bracketed with them.[7] Then Virchow, examining a number of
Lappish skulls at Helsinki, Lund and Copenhagen, in conjunction with ancient Ligurian skulls, discovered many mutual
features suggesting an identical strain. Chief among these was
the under-development of the jaw-bone. The mandible of the
Lapps is always small, the bone-formation unemphasized and
the chin of a receding pattern not exactly repeated in any other
human group – with the very exception of these almost
entirely extinct Ligurians. Ligurians and Lapps both suggested a mountain-dwelling type – in all likelihood, the ancient
reindeer-hunter.

Giuseppe Sergi[8] at a later date maintained that peoples of the
Aryan language group, coming from the east, occupied a zone
of Central Europe north of the Alps, with the result that the
pre-Aryan population split into two branches – Italo-Iberic
and 'Scandinavian'.

Now, none of this quarrels with Virchow's theory that the
descendants of the Iberians and the Ligurians – for instance,
the present-day Sardinians – had betrayed some characteristic
features of the ancient populations who were pre-Aryan in
language.

Anthropological theory had until then restricted the area inhabited by Palæo-Europeans of Lapponoid type; later developments greatly expanded it. It came to be tentatively held that in
very remote times a large sector of Europe had been inhabited
by a homogenous race, which the anthropologist De Quatre-
fages defined with no hesitation as 'Lapponic'. With the in-
cursions of the Indo-European peoples into Europe, this
original race was driven into the mountains – the Pyrenees and
the Alps – and we may assume that the last nuclei of hunting-
peoples occupying the eastern regions of the Baltic would
similarly be driven northwards into what is now Karelia.

171

W. Z. Ripley was ahead of his time when he divided European populations into a Nordic (or Teutonic) type; a Mediterranean (or Ibero-Insular) type; and finally, the Alpine type (to which Pruner-Bey preferred to give the name 'Lapponoid race'). For the first time, the possibility was admitted that we might be dealing with a people of independent origins, deriving from no other stock.[9] But what is meant by a 'Lapponoid race', and how does this race type differ from others?

It may be said at once that European inhabitants among this group can be very clearly told apart from all others. They are short of stature, but the trunk is fairly long: possibly geographical conditions exerted some influence here, though only towards the intensification of original features. The limbs are short and muscular, hands small and well made; the feet have the high instep to be expected of those who travel great distances on foot; a mountainous and Arctic terrain may have had something to do with this, similar characteristics being the common lot of many races living in similar conditions – the Mordvins, the Eskimos, the North American Indians, and so on. Eyes are generally grey or brown, and it is to be observed particularly that quite often they do not appear completely open, so that the lids are reminiscent of the Mongol type. But the fold in the eye-lid, which is nearly always on the outside edge of the eye (the *epicanthus* form is rare) very probably results from the shape of the orbit – among the Lapps, relatively narrow and set low. Few races at the present time possess this feature. On the other hand, it was fairly common in pre-historic times – still further proof of the antiquity of the Lapp type.

The eyebrows are protuberant and not close-set, the nose pointed and concave but not wide. The wide, low face (for which Bryn[10] gives the index-figure 81·2) is somewhat exceptional in Europe – the type is more frequent in tropical and southern regions. The hair is dark and smooth; in certain zones, however, it is quite often fair.

The cranium tends to be well-rounded, with low and narrow eye-sockets (Cephalic index over 80, on average under 86), so that the type may be regarded as brachycephalic. It is easily distinguishable from the North Germanic Dolico-cephalic; less easily from the Mediterranean type.

A number of authorities, among them Müller in 1879, and Haeckel between 1879 and 1900, attempted a systematization of human stocks on a basis of a combined linguistic and an-thropological approach. But with J. Deniker (1900),[11] we return to classification by physical features pure and simple. Deniker's first broad sub-divisions proceed by the criteria of hair, examined for nature and form, skin-pigmentation, nasal and cranial indices, and stature. The Lapps on this reckoning come to be grouped with the 'Ugric race'. Deniker finds grounds for relating them to the Turco-Tataric group – a hazardous claim perhaps. They remain, on the other hand, quite distinct from the Mongols. This reversion to a theory of Asiatic origins (though this time it left the Lapps unconnected with the Mongolian stocks) by a man of Deniker's reputation once more started a great deal of discussion. Not all scholars could accept the premises from which he argued his case. He held that the main differentiations between physical racial characteristics came into being once and for all. His whole-hearted acceptance of this idea is implicit in the deductions he is led to make when establishing common origins for divergent race-groups. Yet many authorities felt that there was not sufficient evidence for his claims and their response was negative.

Anthropologists, biologists, and even geographers, now joined forces in their search for a solution based on a biological and geographical race-succession system, and one of the sources they went back to was F. Ratzel, who had made special studies of peoples whose zone of habitation had been dictated by their need for flight or retreat.

This led to a division into 'protomorph' or primitive 'archemorph', recent; and 'metamorph', mixed.

The Dutch Doctor C. H. Stratz started from the premise – which had already received support from Virchow – that before the immigrations of races of Indo-European language, Europe was populated over a large area by a racial type with a markedly round cranium. At the beginning of the century, he formulated the theory that the Lapps constituted the ultimate survivors of this prehistoric race, which stemmed in its turn from an ancient root-stock, the progenitor of both white and yellow peoples.[12] Stratz pronounced the Lapps a 'meta-morphic' race (that is white $\times$ yellow). In 1906, Renato Biasutti[13] rebelled against this label as applied to present-day races, giving them instead his own description of 'proto-morphic'; for surely, he argued, these old-established groups showed little tendency towards change, their very geographical setting being a guarantee of continual racial purity. This must certainly apply to the Lapps. They were less primitive than other races but they occupied a backwater of Europe, having been forced into it. They appeared to Biasutti, who has recently declared that he still stands by the view he expressed a good many years ago, as 'an old endemic pattern, developed under the peculiar isolating conditions' of the Arctic tundra.[14]

Recently, the Swiss ethnologist George Montandon has propounded his famous theory of ologenesis: the human starting-point, he holds, was a global one, in the sense that one branch of a given species reaches a certain point of evolution and then disappears, giving rise to two new forms deriving from it. It is obvious that in the passing of thousands of years of human history, a vast number of racial types will have arisen and only a few survived. In Montandon's view, 'Lapponoids' and Europoids form the two by-products of the original Europoid stock, to use the term in its strict sense. More precisely, the Lapponoids represent the more precocious element of this twin offspring, and the Europoids the tardier one.[15] Montandon then proceeds to examine the origin of the Lapps from the point of view of their material and spiritual culture, in the light of a journey made among the Ainu inhabitants of Sakhalin and Ieso. His is an important contribution to the study of Arctic cultures, and his theory of ologenesis has yielded surprising results.

Stratz's outworn theory, which made the Lapps the descendants of an encounter between white and yellow, and a metamorphic race, was abandoned by all subsequent authorities. But then, within certain limits, it was taken up again by the Swede K. B. Wiklund.[16] Wiklund conceded the possibility of survival of one primitive branch of an otherwise extinct stock, in which PalæoAsiatic and PalæoEuropean features were blended. In other words, he believed that a group of tribes of such origins, surprised by some natural phenomenon like the last Ice Age, remained imprisoned within the bounds of a limited region like northern Scandinavia. Cut off from all contact with other peoples it stayed there for thousands of years, and survived.

K. E. Schreiner[17] claimed that the Lapps belonged to an ancient stock which produced Asiatic and Alpine peoples alike. But he found himself facing strong opposition from other authorities who questioned the validity of his bloodgroupings of the two types. And here his opponents were right: more recent study has proved that similarities in the bloodgroup do not necessarily prove consanguinity between racial stocks which are geographically remote from each other.

In a second edition of his works published in 1937, E. von Eickstedt[18] gives us a general picture of the various races of man which is symmetrical and complete. He postulates a subspecies, *Homo sapiens albus,* of various series and under series C (brachymorphic) groups four types. The first of these he categorizes as *Homo sapiens alpinus:* it includes Alpine peoples and the Lapps. This marks a return to the views of earlier authorities, but still leaves unanswered a question of prime importance when we are grouping the two stocks together: are we entitled to consider the isolated Alpine ethnic groups still to be found living in Europe's mountain ranges as being of equally ancient origin as the reindeer-peoples of Scandinavia?

B. Lundman[19] has done excellent work of research and synthesis on questions of racial origins. Examining blood-groups, he pronounces the Lapps to be of pure Western-European stock – with the reservation that the inhabitants of eastern Lapland (the Kola peninsula and USSR territory) probably have some admixture of the Samoyed. It is worth recording, too, that Lundman casts some doubts on Wiklund's theory of the Lapps' 'winter sojourn' in Scandinavia during the Ice Age. He inclines rather to the belief that they arrived in the north, for the first time, in the wake of the receding ice.

To sum up, the gist of modern speculation on Lappish origins is that they do bear some ethnic relationship to Alpine stocks and to the various groups which, still in possession of many pre-Aryan characteristics, by reason of their geographical isolation survive in the Europe of today.

It is Biasutti[20] who has the last word – at least chronologically speaking. He considers the Lapp race to be 'appreciably autonomous, such differentiation as exists being attributable to environmental peculiarities'. In other words, the Lapps are admittedly different: the conditions of their life in the far north are unimaginably remote from our own and their appearance evokes a more ancient world. But for all that, they are rooted in the greater branch of Europoid peoples.

Notes

1 F. Negri, *Viaggio Settentrionale*, Padua, 1700

2 K. B. Wiklund, *Prehistory of the Lapps*, Stockholm, 1932

1 W. J. Raudonikas, *Les Gravures rupestres des bords du lac Onega et de la Mer Blanche*, Leningrad, 1936–8.
2 E. Manker, Zur Frage nach dem Alter der Rennzucht, in *Zeitschrift für Ethonologie*, 79, 2, Brunswick, 1954.
3 G. Hallström, *Förhistoria, Arkeologi och Forminnen i Sverige*, Stockholm, 1924.
4 P. L. Zambotti, *Le più antiche civiltà nordiche*, Milan, 1941.
5 E. Manker, *De svenska fjällapparna*, Stockholm, 1947.
6 E. Manker, Zur Frage nach dem Alter der Rennzucht, in *Zeitschrift für Ethonologie*, 79, 2, Brunswick, 1954.
7 K. B. Wikulnd, *Prehistory of the Lapps*, Stockholm, 1932.
8 A. Björn, *Nogen morske stenaldersproblemer*, Oslo, 1929.
9 V. Tanner, *Skolt Lapparna, Antropogeogr. Studier*, Helsinki, 1929.
10 G. Gjessing, Circumpolar Stone Age, in *Acta Artica* II, Copenhagen, 1944.

CHAPTER II

11 Tacitus, *Germania*, XLVI, 3.
12 E. Manker, *De svenska fjällapparna*, Stockholm, 1947.
13 Procopius, *The Goths* II, 15; *History of the Wars*, Vol. 5, 6, 7.
14 F. Negri, *Viaggio settentrionale*, Padua, 1700.
15 Jordanes, *De origine actibusque Getarum*, III, 5.
16 Paulus Diaconus, *Historia Langobardorum*.
17 E. Manker, *De svenska fjällapparna*, Stockholm, 1947.

M

The Lapps

CHAPTER III

18 Saxo Grammaticus (Sakses), *Danesaga* I–IV, Copenhagen, 1925.
19 E. Manker, *De svenska fjällapparna,* Stockholm, 1947.
20 Olaus Magnus, *Historia de gentibus septentrionalibus,* Rome, 1555.
21 F. Negri, *Viaggio settentrionale,* Padua, 1700.
22 J. Schefferus, *Lapponia,* Frankfurt, 1673.
23 K. Leem, *Beskrivelse over Finmarkens Lapper,* Copenhagen, 1767.

PART TWO
CHAPTER VI

1 Paulus Diaconus, *Historia Langobardorum.*
2 Olaus Magnus, *Historia de gentibus septentrionalibus,* Rome, 1555.
3 J. Schefferus, *Lapponia,* Frankfurt, 1673.
4 F. Negri, *Viaggio settentrionale,* Padua, 1700.
5 E. Manker, *De svenska fjällapparna,* Stockholm, 1947.
6 F. Negri, *Viaggio settentrionale,* Padua, 1700.

CHAPTER VII

7 Hugo A. Bernatzik, *Lapland,* London, 1938.
8 E. Manker, *De svenska fjällapparna,* Stockholm, 1947.
9 R. Biasutti, *Razze e Popoli della Terra,* vol. I, Turin, 1953.
10 E. Manker, Zur Frage nach dem Alter der Rennzucht, in *Zeitschrift für Ethnologie,* 79, 2, Brunswick, 1954.

CHAPTER VIII

11 G. Montandon, *La civilisation aínou,* Paris, 1937.
12 E. Manker, *Rajden gar. Skogslapparna i Vittangi,* Stockholm, 1934.

PART THREE
CHAPTER XI

1 K. Tiren, Die lappische Volksmusik, in *Acta Lapponica,* Stockholm, 1947.

WORKS OF SPECIAL INTEREST IN THE STUDY OF THE BEAR CULT AND
OTHER CULTS AMONG ARCTIC PEOPLES

K. Rasmussen, *Intellectual Culture of the Caribou Eskimos,* Copenhagen, 1929.

J. Batchelor, *The Ainu of Japan,* New York, 1898.

L. Frobenius, *Kulturgeschichte Afrikas,* Zurich, 1933.

E. Bächler, *Das alpine Paläolithikum der Schweiz,* Basel, 1940.

K. Hörmann, Die Petershöle bei Velden, in *Naturhist. Gesell.* Nuremberg, 1923–33.

R. Rattaglia, La grotto della Pocala, in *Bollett. Paletn. Ital.* VI, 1953.

L. Franz, *Die älteste Kultur der Tschechoslowakei,* Prague, 1936.

P. Laviosa Zambotti, *Le più antiche civiltà nordiche,* Milan, 1941.

G. Montandon, *La civilisation aïnou,* Paris, 1937.

PART FOUR

CHAPTER XIV

1 C. Linnaeus, *Iter lapponicum,* Uppsala, 1913.

2 J. Blumenbach, *Handbuch der verglichen Anatomie und Phisiologie,* Göttingen, 1804

3 S. Nilsson, *Skandinaviska nordens ur-invänare,* Stockholm, 1866.

4 R. Virchow, in J. Ranke: *Der Mensch,* 1885.

5 Reply of J. Ranke: *op. cit.*

6 J. Ranke, *op. cit.*

7 P. Topinard, *Eléments d'anthropologie générale,* Paris, 1885.

8 G. Sergi, *Gli Arii in Europa e in Asia,* Turin, 1903.

9 W. Z. Ripley, *The Races of Europe,* London, 1900.

10 H. Bryn, Norwegische Samen, in *Mitteilungen der anthropologischen Gesellschaft,* LXII, Vienna, 1932.

11 J. Deniker, *Les races et les peuples de la Terre,* Paris, 1900.

12 C. H. Stratz, *Naturgeschichte des Menschen,* Stuttgart, 1904.

13 R. Biasutti, *Situazione e spazio delle province antropologiche nel Mondo Antico,* Florence, 1906.

14 R. Biasutti, *Razze e Popoli della Terra,* Turin, 1953–6.

15 G. Montandon, *L'ologénèse humaine,* Paris, 1928.

16 K. B. Wiklund, *Prehistory of the Lapps,* Stockholm, 1932.

17 K. E. Schreiner, *Zur Osteologie der Lappen*, Oslo, 1935.

18 E. Von Eickstedt, *Rassenkunde und Rassengechichte der Menschheit*, Stuttgart, 1937.

19 B. Lundman, Ergebnisse der anthropologischen Lappenforschung, in *Anthropos*, Posieux, 1952.

20 R. Biasutti, *Razze e Popoli della Terra*, Turin, 1953–6.

Select Bibliography

In writing this book the author has drawn on a large number of sources, and these works are given in the notes on the text (pages 177–80). There is no need to repeat them here. In addition, there are numerous travellers' accounts published in English, of which perhaps the best are:

ACERBI, JOSEPH, *Travels through Sweden, Finland and Lapland to the North Cape in the Years 1798 and 1799*, 2 vols., London, 1802.

BERNATZIK, HUGO ADOLPH, *Lapland*, London, 1937.

CHAPMAN, OLIVE MURRAY, *Across Lapland*, 2nd ed., London, 1948.

DU CHAILLU, PAUL B., *The Land of the Midnight Sun*, 2 vols., London, 1881.

GOURLIE, NORAH, *A Winter with Finnish Lapps*, London, 1939.

The following two books are by writers who have lived among the Lapps, and recorded their experiences:

NEWHOUSE, JOHN, *Reindeer are Wild Too*, London, 1952.

NORDSTRÖM, ESTER BLENDA, *Tent Folk of the Far North*, London, 1930.

From the plentiful supply of scientific literature on the subject which has come out in recent years, the following English-language publications may be mentioned:

COLLINDER, BJÖRN, *The Lapps*, Princeton, 1949.

GJESSING, GUTORM, Changing Lapps, *Monographs on Social Anthropology*, London, 1954.

MANKER, ERNST, The Nomadism of the Swedish Mountain Lapps, *Acta Lapponica*, VII, Stockholm, 1953.

NESHEIM, ASBJÖRN, (ed.), Traits from Life in a Sea-Lappish District, *Nordnorske Samlinger*, VI, Oslo, 1949.

NICKUL, KARL, The Skolt Lapp Community Suenjelsijd during the Year 1938, *Acta Lapponica*, V, Stockholm, 1948.

PAINE, ROBERT, Coast Lapp Society, Vol. I, *Tromsø Museums Skrifter* IV, Tromsø, 1957.

PEHRSON, ROBERT N., *The Bilateral Network of Social Relations in Könkämä Lapp district*, Indiana University Publications, Slavic and East European Series V, Bloomington, Ind., 1957.

WHITAKER, IAN, Social Relations in a Nomadic Lappish Community, *Samiske Samlinger*, II, Oslo, 1955.

Several of these works have comprehensive bibliographies including the titles of many valuable articles in periodicals, etc. Two other outstanding works, written by Lapps, should be listed:

TURI, JOHAN, *Turi's Book of Lappland*, London, 1931.

TURI, JOHAN AND TURI, PER, Lappish texts, *Mémoires de l'Académie royale des sciences et des lettres de Danemark*, Ser. 7, Vol. IV: 2, Copenhagen, 1920.

The photographs for the plates are by the following: Ernst Manker: 1, 3, 5, 6, 9, 12, 14–16, 19, 20, 29. Signor Piero Casarini: 4, 11, 21. The Riwkin Agency, Stockholm: 10. Reportagebild Agency, Stockholm: 13 (this and the preceding photo belong to the archives of A. Mondadori, Editore). The author: 2, 17, 18.

The maps are based on drawings by Signor Paolo Colombo; figures 5, 7, 8–12, 15, 30–3, 40–51, 53, 54 are the result of collaboration between Signor Paolo Colombo, Signorina Carla Rincato and the author. The remaining drawings are adapted from the following authors: W. J. Raudonikas: 4, 29. F. R. Martin: 6. G. Gjessing: 10. E. Manker: 13, 23, 25, 26, 37. G. Berg: 14. J. Schefferus: 16–20. K. Leem: 21. A. Leroi-Gourhan: 22, 28, 35, 38, 39. J. Ranke: 27. K. Nickul: 34. K. B. Wiklund: 55.

2

3

4

9

11

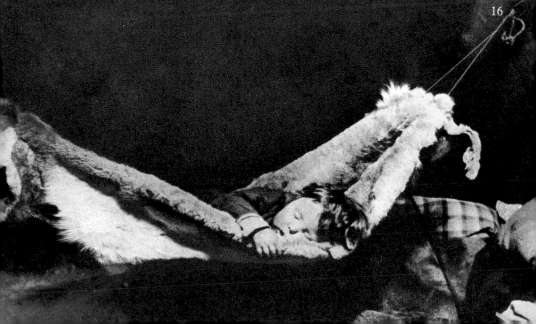

17

18

22

23

25

26

27

Notes on the Plates

1 A rock-drawing in the Flatruet district (near Mittådalen, Swedish Lapland). In the centre are two elk, and above and below are reindeer. Those at the top are partially superimposed.

2 Wood-carvings from the Kola peninsula (USSR) of reindeer with antlers of greatly exaggerated size. Similar artistic licence is found in Magdalenian art of the Palæolithic Age. The holes in this panel suggest that it was once hung up as a decoration. It is in the Nordiska Museum, Stockholm.

3 Vessels exhibited in the Nordiska Museum, Stockholm. On the top row are milking vessels; on the second, plates; on the third, cheese dishes with traditional decoration, not unlike the patterns found among some Arctic-Asiatic peoples; the central motif of the Lappish decorative theme is generally a cross. Bottom row: two bottles and various jars. All these vessels are worked in wood.

4 Lappish skis in the Nordiska Museum, Stockholm. On the left: two prehistoric skis discovered at Lomsjökullen and Sattajärvi, dated to between 1500 and 1200 B.C. by pollen-analysis. The five more recent skis to their right are longer, narrower, and not raised at the centre to take the foot. However, Lappish skis of all epochs have one feature in common – namely the point at both ends.

5 A woman in old-style Lappish costume at Fjellheim, Riasten district, Norway. The stiff, high collar is open in front, and has lace hemming. Some of the metallic ornaments have little bells attached, as worn among many peoples of the steppe from the most ancient times. The Scythians of southern Russia and Siberia adorned their dress with similar little metal plaques, engraved with pictures of animals, in the fifth and fourth centuries B.C.

O

6 A Lapp noted for his prowess at wolf-hunting at Glen, northern Sweden. Wolves are hunted whenever the necessity arises. If they come too close to the village or the reindeer-herd someone will put on a pair of skis and go after them, armed with a kind of iron-tipped pike – or in an emergency, merely with ski-sticks, which are often iron-pointed for this purpose.

7 An old Lapp woman selling skins at a market in northern Norway.

8 The purer Lappish types have no trace of Mongol features. The eyes open in the normal European fashion, the nose is well shaped, not thick, and – a Lappish characteristic – is rounded at the tip.

9 Bride and bridegroom on their way to their wedding. The groom goes bare-headed; the bride wears the head-dress of her particular district. By ancient custom the bridesmaids each wear a large white kerchief with long fringes, which covers their heads underneath their berets and falls over their shoulders.

10 A Lapp from Karesuando – a village on the Finnish-Swedish frontier north of the 68th parallel – photographed at Ritsemjokk, which is farther south. Many Lapps used to migrate with their reindeer from Sweden into Norway, but with the closing of the frontier a few decades ago they had to find new grazing-grounds in order to allow the animals to continue their seasonal migrations between mountain and plain. These they found a good way south of their native district.

11 A reindeer-breeder of Åggojokk, in the Lappish district of Saarivuoma, wearing a skin winter-cape of ancient pattern; the collar is made from the softest and warmest fur, that of young reindeer.

12 Two Lapps drink coffee before striking camp. The tent has already been stripped of skins; the tent poles will be left behind if the country is comparatively well wooded, otherwise they will be loaded on the reindeer. In the background lie the reindeer-packs ready for loading. Around the fire-place are the branches over which skins had been placed to form a couch.

13 Oat-cakes, which take the place of bread, being cooked on old-fashioned bake-stone at Parkajaure, Sweden. Flour has of course to be bought in the villages. At one time it was little known, but now it is more and more in demand, even among nomad groups.

14 Young married woman weaving on the little hand-loom found among all Lappish groups. Its most notable product is banding and braiding of multi-coloured wool, used to decorate capes and berets, or as an edging for shoes to ensure a tight fit round the ankle to keep out snow. Favourite colours are red, yellow and blue.

15 Cradle of a northern local type, at Strimasund in the Lappish district of Umbyn, Sweden. Its ribbons are multi-coloured and decorated with silver and rows of pearls. Until recently the place of these pearls would have been taken by amulets (generally iron) or brooches, and sometimes by knives or arrow-heads, to keep off evil spirits. The sides of the cradle are of reindeer skin, dressed and given scraper-treatment. The baby sleeps on soft skins from the throat of young reindeer.

16 Interior of a cabin at Kroktjarnvallen, in the Jämtland district, Sweden. The child sleeps in a skin hammock slung between two poles.

17 After erecting the tent-poles, a Lapp hoists the skins. The woman is already inside the tent kindling a fire, and from the horizontal pole the cauldron will soon be hanging on a chain. Slung on a tree branch is the baggage, still unpacked. The pack is oval-shaped, as always for reindeer-transportation.

18 Snow-bound Lappish camp at Jokkmokk. The opening in the tent roof gives egress to the smoke. In winter a forest-clearing is a favourite tent-site as trees afford some protection from the wind.

19 Log-cabins at Geijaure, in the forest-district of Mausjaur, Sweden. They are pyramid-shaped on a square base, with a sunken floor, built on typical Eurasiatic lines, uniting the square or rectangular pattern with the conicial Clearly visible is the hole in the roof for the escape of smoke. The door

of the cabin farther from camera seen open, is of the same type as those of the turf cabins.

20 Cupola-form turf cabin with pole framework in the Lappish village of Jukkasjärvi, Sweden. Above the roof-aperture is a framework of branches over which some sort of cover can be placed in rough weather.

21 A *njâllâ* or storage-hut for food, at the Lapp village of Jukkasjärvi, Sweden. These huts were common in ancient times throughout the whole Nordic-Uralic region of Europe, and are clearly reminiscent of a Siberian type of dwelling. Until a few years ago they were frequently seen in Lapland, but now they are rare even among the nomadic groups: only a few Lapps of the Kola peninsula still use them. They were erected and filled at 'halts' in a migration-trek, and the group would return to them again in the following spring.

22 An 'idol' called Tjaltokerke, which returned after fifty-three years absence to its original site, at Tjalmejaure in the Lappish district of Svaipa, Sweden. Lapps believed that certain stones possessed supernatural powers – perhaps inhabited by spirits of the dead which could find no peace, or even as mediums of gods.

23 A *gar'de* or pen formed by stakes to enclose reindeer for marking and other purposes. A turf cabin is seen in the background.

24 A large stag on the eve of losing his antlers. The skin on his horns becomes gradually detached, and will soon fall. At this period the animals become liable to attack people. The reindeers' antlers are asymmetrical, and males have one or two special horns at the front, which may be to shield their eyes in the fierce fights that take place at the rutting season.

25 Image of a Lapp divinity carved in wood, in the Nordiska Museum, Stockholm. Francesco Negri, as long ago as the end of the seventeenth century, discovered a kind of sanctuary in northern Lapland containing many wooden images of this type.

26 Another figure, also in the Nordiska Museum, with characteristic X – markings. Such markings were noted by Francesco Negri in the seventeenth century. They probably bear some relation to the schematic representations of the sun to be seen on a number of shaman's drums in the same museum.

27 Magic drum in the Statens Historiska Museum, Stockholm. This drum, with the one in the note following, was described by Schefferus in 1673 as belonging to the collection of Chancellor Magnus Gabriel de la Gardie. Very probably it came from the Lule district in Sweden. A similar drum was described by Samuel Rheen, Pastor of Jokkmokk, in 1671.

28 Another drum, in the same museum, of which we also have a description by Schefferus (1673). Subsequently, it became the property of the antiquarian Johan Hadorph who left a note on it in a catalogue he compiled in 1690, and then passed into the hands of a second antiquarian Johan Peringskiöld, who described it in 1720. It is considered to be one of the most beautiful Lapp drums in existence and is also among the best preserved.

29 Woman's vest from Lycksele, Sweden. The traditional sun-motifs and geometrical designs decorating the middle of the garment are often encountered on household utensils, and at one time would also be found on weapons.

Index